LONDON
Atlas of Architecture

Alejandro Bahamón

BATSFORD

First edition:
© September 2006, Parramón Ediciones, S. A.
Exclusive publishing rights for all the world.
Ronda de Sant Pere, 5, 4ª planta
08010 Barcelona (Spain)
Company belonging to the Grupo Editorial Norma de América Latina

www.parramon.com

First printed in the United Kingdom in 2007 by

Batsford
10 Southcombe Street
London W14 0RA

An imprint of Anova Books Company Ltd

Pre-printing:
PACMER, S.A

ISBN: 9780713490725
Printed in China

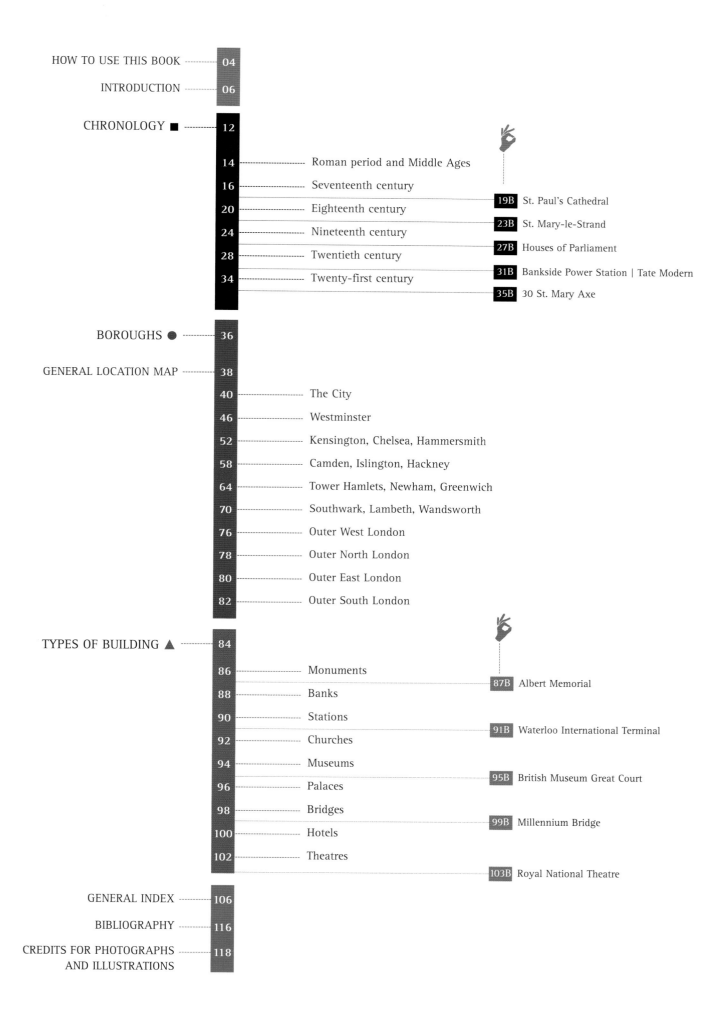

How to use this book

This Atlas of Architecture is intended to guide the reader through the history of the city's architecture by means of three clearly defined sections: Chronology, Boroughs and Types of Building. Each one is represented by a different colour and a specific symbol, making it easy to pinpoint the various buildings on the location maps.

■ CHRONOLOGY

The images and texts in the top part of the timeline explain the most relevant historic events that have affected the city's urban development. The lower part of the timeline contains a selection of the most relevant buildings from each period, illustrated by means of a colour photograph, credits and a brief descriptive text. Each building has a reference that can be used to find it on the map of its corresponding borough in the section BOROUGHS. Each historical period has a zoom, consisting of a double-page foldout that explores one of the buildings from that era in depth.

1–

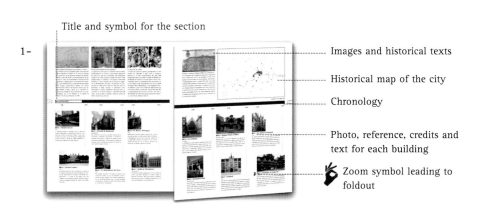

Title and symbol for the section

Images and historical texts

Historical map of the city

Chronology

Photo, reference, credits and text for each building

Zoom symbol leading to foldout

2–

3–

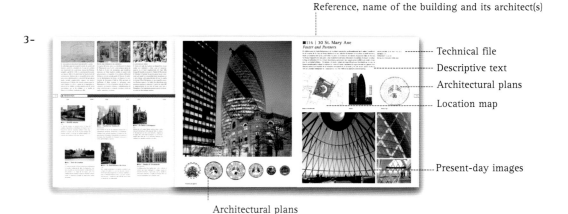

Reference, name of the building and its architect(s)

Technical file

Descriptive text

Architectural plans

Location map

Present-day images

Architectural plans

● BOROUGHS

Each of the boroughs that form London is illustrated by a general map with indications of all the buildings corresponding to it that are referred to in the book. The historical images in the top section illustrate the historical development of each area, while the lower section presents the most important places by means of an image and a descriptive text.

Title and symbol for the section

Illustrations and historical images

Location map of the borough

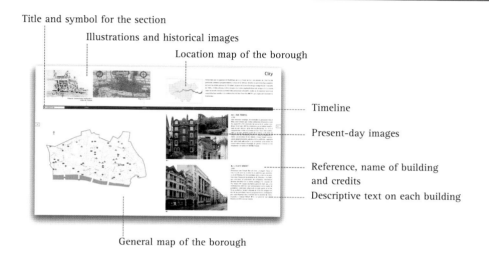

Timeline

Present-day images

Reference, name of building and credits

Descriptive text on each building

General map of the borough

▲ TYPES OF BUILDING

A brief historical review is used to introduce the evolution of each one of the 'Types of Buildings' (museums, theatres, stations, bridges, etc). A selection of the most representative examples of each of the types are explained with a colour photograph, credits and descriptive text. The zooms, which are a double fold-out spreads, study particular buildings in depth.

Title and symbol for the section

Types of building

1—

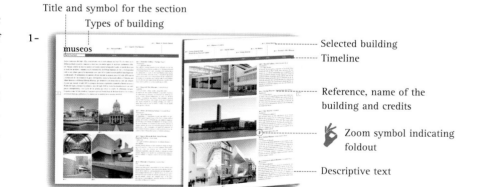

Selected building
Timeline

Reference, name of the building and credits

Zoom symbol indicating foldout

Descriptive text

3—

Technical file
Descriptive text

Location plan

Present-day images

Architectural plans

Architectural plans

CHRONOLOGY

BOROUGHS

TYPES OF BUILDING

Buildings referred to in the CHRONOLOGY chapter

Buildings referred to in the BOROUGHS chapter

Buildings referred to in the TYPES OF BUILDING chapter

Introduction

Since time immemorial, the proximity of water has been one of the basic premises for the establishment of a city. London, like Paris, Vienna, Baghdad, Shanghai, Montreal and so many others, grew up alongside a river that guaranteed a means of communications and a supply of water. The Romans who invaded the island of Britain in the 1st century AD recognised the strategic value of this stretch of the River Thames, and they joined its banks with a pioneering bridge that would be the sole witness to the comings and goes of London's legendary boatmen for over fifteen hundred years. In the 5th century, the Roman settlement, on the site of what is now the City, succumbed to the Saxon hordes from the north who, despite over six centuries of domination, have barely left any architectural traces in London – with the notable exception of Westminster Abbey, which the Normans, on their arrival in Britain in the 11th century, would turn into the hub of the country's political life. The Norman invaders enriched the city's limited architectural heritage by bringing over the Romanic style from the Continent. This evolved into the vibrant English Gothic style that can still be seen today on some buildings in London. The Tudor period witnessed a flourishing of commerce

and the arts, particularly the theatre, as well as the establishment of the boundaries to the great parks that act as the capital's lungs. The year 1666 saw crucial changes in the appearance of London, as the Great Fire that devastated the City in that year triggered a reconstruction that would draw on the principal models of classical architecture. This influence would continue to make itself felt in the following three centuries, which were marked by an expansion of the city in the form of orderly residential neighbourhoods with rows of terrace houses. These new areas were interconnected by an emblematic suburban Underground and train network. In this modern incarnation, London had to recover once again from destruction, this time caused by the German bombing of World War II. The strength that led the British capital forward at that time has remained in evidence until today: London has proved capable of reinventing itself as a polyhedral city acclaimed for its ability to innovate while also treasuring links with the past, comfortable in its dual role as a touchstone for modernity and a safeguard of tradition.

The great conurbation of London is divided into 33 boroughs, spread over a total area of 1,503 sq. km (580 sq. miles). Some 30 percent of this expanse is made up of parks and gardens, making London the city with the most green space in the world. The capital started and finished the 20th century with roughly the same population – seven million – but this

figure fluctuated enormously over the course of those hundred years, not only in terms of overall numbers but also with respect to its composition. In 2001, 29% of Londoners belonged to non-indigenous ethnic groups, in some cases concentrated in specific neighbourhoods where they maintain their cultural traditions. London is one of the richest cities in Europe, with major deals being struck in the City and the relative new Canary Wharf, where many major banks and media companies have their headquarters. The considerable income brought in by tourism must also be taken into account, as the city attracts over 27 million visitors a year. The port, in contrast, has now lost its significant role in the British economy – and, therefore, in the morphology of the capital – in favour of the docks in Tilbury, to the east of Greater London, and elsewhere.

Owing to its pre-eminent position in its own country, in Europe and the world itself over the course of centuries, the multicultural London of today, the great survivor, has been chosen as the city to launch this collection of *Atlases of Architecture.* The complexity of London's history is clearly apparent in the first part of the book, 'Chronology', where the distinctive format of this section makes it possible to focus individually on the many events that have moulded the face of the city, in parallel with the construction of its architectural icons. The specific personality of each of the boroughs that have emerged at various points in history to

complement the initial core of the City is reflected in the section 'Boroughs', with detailed descriptions of the most interesting sites in each administrative division. Finally, London's status as a capital city, along with the infinite diversity of its population, have helped create the appearance of numerous emblematic buildings for public use, such as stations, theatres, churches and bridges, and these are duly described in the section 'Types of Building'.

This *Atlas of Architecture* presents the city in a new light as a result of the book's unusual approach, revolving around the three fields of Chronology, Boroughs and Types of Building. This innovative structure also offers the reader a simultaneous view of the particular and the overall, so that the individual parts – nearly 300 projects with full-colour illustrations – facilitate the understanding of the whole, be it the history of the city, its heterogeneous administrative composition or the main categories of its constructions. The wide range of historical and location maps – as well as the continuous presence of the chronological guide – guarantees this inter-relationship between the architectural works and the geographical and historical context in which they were built, allowing the reader to benefit from a panoramic overview of the historical evolution of the city's architecture, from that first Roman bridge to the cutting-edge skyscrapers being planned for the London of the future.

A STRATEGIC SETTLEMENT FOR ROMANS AND SAXONS

London's strategic geographical position on the banks of the Thames made it the most important crossroads for the Romans when they occupied the province of Britain in 43 AD. The construction of the first bridge over the river determined the location of the original settlement, which became a prosperous administrative and commercial centre. It has left barely any architectural traces. The Saxons took advantage of the decline of the Roman Empire to invade London in 410 but, despite the city's commercial expansion, the only building of any real significance attributed to them is Edward the Confessor's abbey, which was completed in 1066.

NEW WINDS FROM THE CONTINENT

The capital of the Saxon kingdom extended from Westminster Abbey ■006 in the west to an early church dedicated to Saint Paul in the east. The Normans, who invaded England in 1066, brought with them a new architectural idiom: the Romanic style. Their first defensive building, the Tower of London ■002, was followed by the churches of St. Bartholomew the Great ■004 and St. Pancras ■064. The construction of Westminster Hall ■008 by William Rufus in 1097 accentuated the difference between Westminster and the City: the former, the seat of the Court, became the religious and administrative centre, while the former a commercial and artisanal hub.

THE SPREAD OF THE GOTHIC

By the end of the 11th century, the Gothic style had already made an appearance in a city that was starting to abandon the Romanic. Henry III, influenced by the architectural ferment of the 13th century, ordered Edward the Confessor's Westminster Abbey ■006 to be rebuilt. The simple early Gothic evolved, acquiring greater complexity until it emerged as a robust, perpendicular style, superbly exemplified by Henry VII's chapel in Westminster. Meanwhile, the City had achieved greater political and commercial autonomy. The construction of the Inns of Court between the City and Westminster, in the 14th century, began to reduce the distance between the two areas.

■ CHRONOLOGY

| 220 | 1097 | 1106 | 1123 | 1215 | 1245 |

■001 | Roman wall
City

The Roman wall extended from the Tower of London to Blackfriars, enclosing a total of 3,011 acres. Various fragments of the wall have been preserved near the Tower, with traces of the medieval reconstruction visible on top. These are some of the few surviving vestiges of Roman London.

■003 | Southwark Cathedral
Southwark

This cathedral is one of the rare examples of Norman architecture still to be seen in Southwark. Originally founded as an Augustine priory, it has been partially refurbished and rebuilt on several occasions and is notable for its mixture of English and French Gothic styles.

■005 | St. Helen's, Bishopsgate
City

Apart from being the biggest medieval church to survive both the Great Fire of 1666 and the Blitz, St. Helen's is distinguished by its two adjacent naves, built in the 12th and 13th centuries. Its interior, mainly dating from the 15th century, is distinguished by tombs from the Elizabethan and Jacobean periods.

■002 | Tower of London
Tower Hamlets

The construction of the Tower began shortly after the Norman invasion in 1066. Its imposing mass of Caen stone has undergone considerable modifications over the centuries, but this combination of fortress and palace is still a magnificent example of Norman military architecture.

■004 | St. Bartholomew the Great
City

This Norman building is the oldest monastic church in London. The nave was knocked down when the building passed into private hands after the Anglican reformation. It went on to serve a wide range of secular functions for many years before Sir Aston Webb was commissioned to restore it in the late 19th century.

■006 | Westminster Abbey
Westminster

The building visible today was built between 1245 and 1260 on the site of the old abbey put up by Edward the Confessor. Other elements were added centuries later, including Henry VII's chapel and the towers designed by Hawksmoor on the western façade.

A LONDON TAILOR-MADE FOR HENRY VIII
AND ITS ARISTOCRATS

Demographic growth prompted the city's expansion beyond its walls, although commerce still revolved around the river. The 16th-century Tudor era was characterized by its prosperity, which allowed Henry VIII to alter the face of the capital. On the one hand, the land confiscated from the Church after the breach with Rome was occupied by new palaces and houses; on the other, the creation of royal hunting grounds, such as Hyde Park ●13 and St. James's Park ●11, gave rise to the extensive green area that has been preserved in the city centre until today.

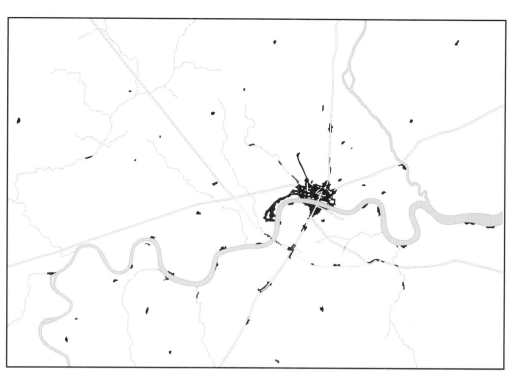

London in the 16th century

1300   1402   1420   1440   1520   1586

■007 | St. Etheldreda's
Camden
St. Etheldreda's is a small chapel once reserved for the private use of the Bishops of Ely, who lived in an adjoining residence now no longer in existence. Two elaborate, imposing stained-glass windows on the east and west façades illuminate this simple volume, which is set back from the street.

■008 | Westminster Hall
Westminster
This hall is set in a building commissioned by Richard II to replace a previous one dating from the 11th century, of which barely any traces remain. The outstanding element in the new nave is the elaborate vaulted wooden structure supporting the roof, which has been renovated on several occasions.

■009 | Bishop's Palace, Fulham
Hammersmith
This building, which on some façades is more reminiscent of a rural vicarage than a palace, was home to the Bishops of London from the 17th to the 19th century. It has been refurbished several times and its main features are the central courtyard, the 18th-century tower and the neo-Gothic chapel.

■010 | Guildhall
City
This seat of local administration, built over two crypts, is one of the few secular medieval buildings still remaining in London, although its roof was rebuilt after the Great Fire and the Blitz. The façade of the courtyard was renovated in 1788, drawing inspiration from classical, Gothic and Indian motifs.

■011 | St. Andrew Undershaft
City
St. Andrew Undershaft numbers among the handful of medieval churches that emerged unscathed from both the Great Fire of 1666 and the German bombardments. The splendid renaissance doorway leads on to an attractive interior that has acquired ornamentation over the centuries as a result of donations made by parishioners ▲52.

■012 | Houses on Staple Inn
Camden
These houses represent the most outstanding example of 16th-century domestic architecture in London. They are characterised by distinctive façades with a mesh of woodwork, rows of windows, projections on the first-floor pillars and the double-slope roof.

A LONDON FOR EVERY SOCIAL CLASS

In the 17th century, the bustling city centre was taken over by traders, who lived in tumbledown wooden houses built on the medieval urban configuration. A single bridge connected the north with the south bank, where the leisure activities were concentrated: theatre, cockfights and public executions. The precarious sewage system meant that epidemics were a constant threat. The disposal of waste into the Thames repelled the nobles and merchants, who preferred to settle in outlying areas like Richmond, Hampstead and Highgate.

NEW ARCHITECTS FOR A NEW STYLE

The Renaissance represented a cultural and artistic renewal in which the individual ousted God as the centre of the universe. Although England's literary output in the 16th century was already clearly steeped in this new ideology, it was not until the following century that the Renaissance made an impact on architecture. Up until then, this discipline had remained in the hands of master craftsmen employed by the Crown or the Church. Humanism spurred the emergence of the new concept of an architect well versed in all the arts, with Inigo Jones and Christopher Wren as its standard bearers.

INIGO JONES

Born into a humble family, Jones (1573–1652) travelled widely in Italy as a young man, enabling him to soak up the new ideas of Humanism. After gaining royal favour on his return to London, he was commissioned to build the new banqueting hall in Whitehall ■016. Jones was intimately acquainted with the work of Palladio (whose *Quattro Libri dell'Architettura* he had annotated in 1601) and in 1622 he completed the first classical building to be put up in the centre of London. From then on his designs, exemplified above all by the Covent Garden Piazza of 1630 ●14, were taken as a model for several generations of English architects.

■ CHRONOLOGY

1606	1607	1616	1619	1623	1628

■013 | Globe Theatre

Southwark

Although the current Globe Theatre is a reconstruction – it was opened to the public in 1997 – it has followed the lines of the original construction. It was the first theatre to be built on Bankside, as part of the leisure activities on offer in this area, and it provides a superb example of London's late medieval architecture ▲80.

■014 | Charlton House

Greenwich

This ancestral home has been preserved in its entirety, along with its corresponding chapel. The E-shape, three-storey building, clad in red brick and decorated with white stone, is fronted by an elaborate porch. Two square towers mark the ends of the longitudinal axis.

■015 | Queen's House, Greenwich

Greenwich
Inigo Jones

This palace, commissioned from Jones by Queen Anne of Denmark, comprised two parallel rectangular volumes joined by a bridge at the level of the first floor. Despite subsequent enlargements, this residence's most striking features are its austerity and the strict Vitruvian proportions typical of early Palladianism. ▲56

■016 | Banqueting House

Westminster
Inigo Jones

The Banqueting House, with a white Portland-stone cladding new at the time, is a rectangular volume with ornamentation, Ionic on the ground floor and Corinthian on the first store. The hall on the upper level has a panelled ceiling decorated by Rubens.

■017 | Queen's Chapel

Westminster
Inigo Jones

A further example of the Palladianism imported by Jones, the Queen's Chapel formed part of St. James's Palace ▲55 until it was separated by the creation of Marlborough Road in the 19th century. It is a building with an austere main façade with an interior dominated by a vaulted coffered ceiling.

■018 | St. Katherine Cree

City

This was one of the few churches to be built in the reign of Charles I. The entrance is set in the tower to the west, dating from the 16th century. Inside, the vaulted ceiling is supported by Corinthian columns that separate the central nave from the two side naves.

TO AND FRO OF THE MONARCHY AND THE REPUBLIC

Although Charles I promoted Palladianism in the first half of the 17th century, his execution in 1649 brought its expansion to a temporary halt. The Civil War barely left its mark on London, apart from the fortifications built in the far west of the city. With the arrival of the Republic, London seemed set to embark on a new era when Cromwell sold the royal family's properties, in the hope of filling the state coffers. Time was not on his side, however, as in just over a decade the monarchy was restored and Charles II retook possession of the Stuart domains.

LONDON RISES UP FROM THE ASHES

The threat of the plague became a reality in the torrid summer of 1665, leaving nearly 100,000 victims in its wake. The following year, fire ran amok in the City: over the course of four days it wiped out 400 streets, destroying over 80 churches and 13,200 houses. Although detailed reconstruction plans were drawn up (inspired by the orderly urban development of the great European cities), the overwhelming need to return to normal led to rebuilding on the medieval configuration, albeit with wood and straw irrevocably spurned in favour of brick and tiles.

CHRISTOPHER WREN

Wren (1632–1723), the epitome of the humanist architect, worked as a professor of astronomy at Oxford before drawing up his first building. Despite being virtually unknown outside academic circles, this mathematician became an active participant in the reconstruction of the city after the Great Fire. Over the course of his career he designed, in addition to St. Paul's Cathedral, 51 new churches, of which less than half are still standing today. His versatility and originality made him the leading figure in the group of classical architects that emerged during the 17th century.

| 1640 | 1650 | 1661 | 1664 | 1670 | 1670 |

■019 | Lindsey House
Camden
Inigo Jones (attributed)
The property developer William Newton built 32 residences around Lincoln Inn's Fields ●35, the first square with a garden in London, but only one of them, Lindsey House, has remained intact to this day. Its design is obviously in the style of Inigo Jones, although his authorship is in doubt; be that as it may, it set a precedent that would be followed for two centuries.

■020 | Gray's Inn
Camden
Gray's Inn, one of the four Inns of Court built from the 14th century onward between the City and Westminster, boasts a large hall with a hammer-beam ceiling, a library and a chapel, which had to be rebuilt after being flattened by the bombardments of 1941.

■021 | Kensington Palace
Kensington
Christopher Wren, Nicholas Hawksmoor,
William Kent, Thomas Ripley (attributed)
In order to escape the pollution of the city, William III moved to Kensington Palace, a Jacobean mansion dating from 1605. Wren transformed the building into a royal residence, while keeping its proportions on a domestic scale, but George I later refurbished it in a style more in keeping with a palace. ▲57

■022 | Royal Naval Hospital
Greenwich
Christopher Wren, Nicholas Hawksmoor,
Sir John Vanbrugh, John Webb
At the instigation of Charles II, Webb designed a new palace comprising three buildings that were to be set around a central courtyard opening on to the river. Only the western wing was completed; decades later, Wren transformed it into a naval hospital. ●46

■023 | St. Mary-le-Bow
City
Christopher Wren
The new tower on this old Norman church, which was built after the rest of the building, provides a magnificent example of ordered classical architecture. After the Blitz, the tower was restored in accordance with Wren's plans, although the interior was substantially modified.

■024 | Leicester Square
Westminster
The Earl of Leicester bought this former grazing land and built Leicester House along its northern edge (the eastern, southern and western sides were not occupied until decades later). The square was urbanised in 1874 and has not preserved any of its original buildings.

THE FLEETING ENGLISH BAROQUE

The baroque style, characterized by voluptuous forms and ornamental opulence, had a short life in England, basically confined to the period between 1690 and 1730. Even at its peak, English baroque was more restrained than its continental versions, but this did not diminish the power of the subsequent neoclassical reaction, the Georgian style. Nicholas Hawksmoor and John Vanbrugh were the main representatives of this movement, each with his own style (the former influenced by the classicism of Wren, the latter more exuberant and uninhibited).

EXPANSION TOWARD THE WEST

After the Great Fire of London in 1666, the wealthier inhabitants built their new family homes in the western part of the city. St. James's Square ●16, Piccadilly and Mayfair had already lost their rural character by the turn of the 18th century, while William III's preference for Kensington and Hampton Court as the site of his royal residences increased the popularity of these areas among the upper classes. The westward expansion was also consolidated by the construction of the new Chelsea Hospital, built at the instigation of Charles II and his niece, Queen Mary.

THE NEW LONDONERS

The east of the city also underwent a transformation in the second half of the 17th century. The urban population continued to grow in leaps and bounds, as the reconstruction process attracted countless craftsmen from all over the country. At the same time, the religious persecution that had begun in France in 1685, after the revocation of the Edict of Nantes, prompted 30,000 Huguenot refugees to flee to London. They settled in Spitalfields and Soho, where some of the garrets in which they set up textile workshops can still be seen today.

■ CHRONOLOGY

| 1670 | 1671 | 1672 | 1675 | 1676 | 1677 |

■025 | St. Lawrence Jewry
City
Christopher Wren
The Guildhall's old church was destroyed in the Great Fire of 1666 but then replaced by a new one designed by Wren. The Corinthian-style eastern façade, clad with Portland stone, is based on that of St. Paul's. The interior was restored after the Blitz, in accordance with the plans drawn up by Wren.

■026 | Monument
City
Christopher Wren, Robert Hooke
This robust Doric column made of Portland stone commemorates the devastating fire that swept through the City in 1666. The 62-m (203-ft) pillar decorated with golden flames rises from a square pedestal. Inside the monument 345, black marble steps climb to a panoramic terrace ▲01.

■027 | St. Stephen Walbrook
City
Christopher Wren
Wren tried out the design for St. Paul's ■028 on the interior of this church. The rectangular ground plan is marked out by 16 columns that divide the building into five naves and free a central area overshadowed by the spectacular coffered vault.

👉 ■028 | St. Paul's Cathedral
City
Christopher Wren
Wren's most famous building, put up on the ruins of the medieval cathedral destroyed by the Great Fire of 1666, kept him busy for almost 40 years. The cathedral is made up of four volumes: the dome plus its cross; the central and side naves; the transepts; and the western end.

■029 | St. James's, Piccadilly
Westminster
Christopher Wren
The longitudinal axis of this rectangular church is emphasised by the row of windows stretching across the north and south elevations, with decorative details in stone alleviating the austerity of their brickwork. The tower was added years later by Wren himself.

■030 | St. Benet, Paul's Wharf
City
Christopher Wren
This small church consists of a simple parallelepiped with a roof sloping down on all four sides and an adjacent tower crowned by a dome and a lead pinnacle. The elevations are decorated with a chequered motif, along with garlands on the windows on the west and south façades.

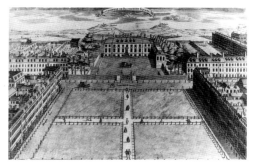

THE BIRTH OF MODERN LONDON

The reconstruction was a boon for property developers, who jumped at the chance to build new residential neighbourhoods like Marylebone and Bloomsbury. The century's most important urban innovation was the square, a semi-public garden surrounded by rows of brick houses. The orderly, spacious layout of the new neighbourhoods contrasted with the dense maze of the City. In just half a century, London had grown from a medieval port with wooden buildings into a classical city dominated by brick.

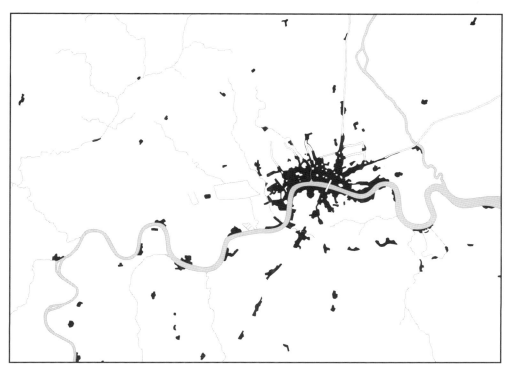

London in the 17th century

1677   1680   1681   1684   1686   1695

■031 | College of Arms
City

Although this was originally a square complex built around a courtyard, one side was removed when the adjoining street was opened up. The façade, with its brickwork left open to view, gives on to the Thames by means of an outdoor gallery.

■032 | St. Augustine
City
Christopher Wren

The bombs of the Blitz were not the first onslaught experienced by this church, as it had already been rebuilt after the Great Fire of 1666. The only survivor of the original building is the tower, which was restored in the 1960s to incorporate it into the adjacent building, the headquarters of the choir of St. Paul's Cathedral.

■033 | Royal Hospital
Kensington
Christopher Wren, Nicholas Hawksmoor, John Vanbrugh

Although the functional model for this hospital was Les Invalides in Paris, its design created a template for institutional architecture that was propagated in numerous countries under British influence. The complex consists of several three-storey wings with exposed brickwork, organised around three open courtyards.

■034 | St. Margaret Pattens
City
Christopher Wren

The tower, situated at the northeast end of the main volume, is the most outstanding element in this simple, square church crowned with a soaring lead pinnacle. The interior of the building has preserved part of its original carpentry.

■035 | St. Michael Paternoster Royal
City
Christopher Wren

This church was destroyed first by the Great Fire of 1666 and then by the Blitz. The first reconstruction was entrusted to Wren, who added a tower culminating in a spectacular octagonal lantern to the austere parallelepiped (geometric solid).

■036 | Morden College
Greenwich
Christopher Wren

This complex, one of the few surviving examples of Wren's civil architecture, was founded by the Turkish merchant John Morden, whose statue dominates the entrance arch. The building is arranged around a square courtyard lined by a Doric colonnade.

■ 028 | St. Paul's Cathedral
Christopher Wren

The project drawn up by Wren to rebuild the cathedral received royal approval in 1675, the year in which the titanic construction work was launched by a substantial team of craftsmen. Two flights of steps by the western entrance lead up to the double-height portico made up of 10 pairs of Corinthian columns flanked by two towers. The lobby offers the magnificent spectacle of the central nave, set off by two lower side naves. Beyond the superb choir stands the high altar, which was rebuilt on several occasions. The huge dome, undoubtedly the cathedral's most emblematic feature, is as wide as the central nave plus the side naves put together, and so it required a complex structure of arches and pillars to support the weight of the drum. The ascent up to the lantern via the Whispering Gallery allows visitors to enjoy a stunning panoramic view of the City.

DISTRICT The City
LOCATION St. Paul's Churchyard, EC4
MAXIMUM HEIGHT 108 m (354 ft)
SURFACE AREA 8,410 sq. m
DATE OF CONSTRUCTION 1675

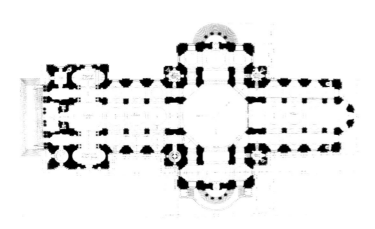
Ground plan

Elevation and section of the bell tower

19B

ast elevation

West elevation

South elevation

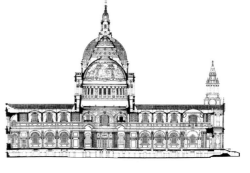

Longitudinal section

PROSPERITY IN THE HANOVERIAN KINGDOM

Between the Utrecht peace treaty in 1713 and the Battle of Waterloo in 1815, Great Britain grew into an international commercial powerhouse. This upsurge was favoured by the relative security and colonial expansion of the reigns of the three Hanoverian Georges (1714–1811), known as the Georgian period. When the Tories came to power, they approved the construction of fifty new churches. The relevant Act of Parliament specified churches made of stone with several towers and steeples, which made it necessary to pursue Wren's efforts to reconcile classical architecture with the typical Christian tower.

A NEW SOCIAL ORDER

London, the splendid capital of the new global superpower, witnessed the emergence of a new social order in the 18th century. On the one hand, the economic boom had enabled merchants to accumulate considerable wealth; on the other, the nobles who had settled in the countryside a hundred years earlier started to show a renewed interest in the city. Finally, craftsmen and shopkeepers sprung up around the *nouveaux riches*, anxious to cater to their every need. Over the course of the 18th century, the population rose from 670,500 to 900,000 in 1801.

THE RESURGENCE OF PALLADIANISM

In the first half of the 18th century, Palladianism became the official style of the upper classes. The rejection of baroque excess led a group of erudite aristocrats to delve afresh into the legacy of Inigo Jones and Andrea Palladio, inspiring Lord Burlington to build his emblematic Chiswick House ■045. The year 1715 saw the publication of two books that established the principles of this classical revival: the *Vitrubius Britannicus* by Colen Campbell, which gathered together the finest classical buildings in England, and the English translation of Palladio's *Quattro Libri*.

■ CHRONOLOGY

| 1709 | 1710 | 1712 | 1712 | 1714 | 1715 |

■037 | Dr. Johnson's House
City

The residence of Doctor Samuel Johnson is of particular interest for its stark and rational configuration, along with the complex around it, centred on Gough Square. Johnson's House is one of the few domestic buildings in the City to have survived from the early 18th century.

■038 | Roehampton House
Wandsworth
Thomas Archer

Despite having been modernised and enlarged to accommodate Queen Mary's Hospital, this old country house has conserved the imposing steps leading to the front door (framed by a redbrick façade), as well as many of its original fireplaces.

■039 | St. Alfege, Greenwich
Greenwich
Nicholas Hawksmoor, John James

This church, the first to be commissioned after the Tories' return to power, established the model for subsequent projects: a central biaxial space and a large oval moulding on the ceiling of the nave. The exterior is distinguished by the surprisingly distant placement of the tower, which was completed by James.

■040 | St. Paul's, Greenwich
Greenwich
Thomas Archer

Archer fulfilled a commission from 1711 with this splendid example of the baroque style. The wide steps leading to the entrance, complete with a Tuscan portico, soften the relationship of the nave with the tower.

■041 | St. Mary-le-Strand
Westminster
James Gibbs

Gibbs' training in Italy enabled him to incorporate elements of the Mannerist style into this church. The main entrance, marked by a semicircular portico, leads to a rectangular interior culminating in an apse with striking stone carvings at the eastern end.

■042 | Burlington House
Westminster
Lord Burlington, Colen Campbell

After his journeys to Italy, Burlington hired Campbell to renovate his London residence in the classical style of Palladio and Inigo Jones. Campbell's intervention has barely survived successive refurbishments of the building, which launched Burlington's campaign to reform contemporary architectural practice.

WILLIAM KENT AND OTHER NEW ARCHITECTS

The profession of architect as we know it today has its origins in the 18th century. Its first champions were Lord Burlington and Sir William Chambers, who personified a finely balanced combination of gentleman, artist and architect. A large group of prestigious professionals grew up around Burlington, headed by his partners Colen Campbell and William Kent. The latter embodied the figure of the universal designer, as he devoted himself to disciplines as diverse as painting, architecture, landscape gardening and furniture design.

LORD BURLINGTON

After travelling to Italy at the age of 20, Richard Boyle (1694–1753), the third Earl of Burlington, set about steering English architecture away from baroque tendencies in order to recover the classical balance of Palladio and Jones. To this end, he surrounded himself with professionals like Colen Campbell, William Kent and John Michael Rysbrack, and together they advocated the return to a style that they considered more appropriate to the new Hanoverian dynasty. The monumental nature of Palladianism quickly won enthusiasm among both the gentry coming in from the country and the emerging middle class of merchants.

THE COLONIES, A SOURCE OF INSPIRATION

The colonial expansion combined with the intercontinental voyages popular among the upper classes to establish contact with other cultures and broaden the horizons of a new generation of architects. Eclecticism made its mark on the architecture of London, where the latest buildings effortlessly combined Palladian principles with neo-Gothic, Indian and Oriental elements. Chambers' Pagoda, the Adam brothers' Syon House and Walpole's Strawberry Hill constitute magnificent examples of the creative freedom evident in the late 18th century.

1717　　1721　　1725　　1730　　1733　　1735

■043 | Royal Arsenal
Greenwich
John Vanbrugh (attributed)
The Royal Arsenal, set in an old military zone that has gone on to be a new residential neighbourhood, is made up of three buildings, of which the Model Room most faithfully represents Vanbrugh's style. The imposing brick entrance decorated with white stone is flanked by two pillars topped with lions.

■044 | St. Martin-in-the-Fields
Westminster
James Gibbs
The urbanisation of Trafalgar Square ●35 made it possible to benefit from the superb view of this church, which is a synthesis of the influences of Rome, Wren and Palladio. Its square tower, which culminates in a highly wrought pinnacle, stands behind a portico made up of six Corinthian columns and a frontispiece. The interior is distinguished by the exquisite plasterwork on the ceiling.

■045 | Chiswick House
Hunslow
Lord Burlington
Burlington was inspired by Palladio's Villa Capra when he designed himself this country house close to his family home. The octagonal vault standing out from the roof is the most striking feature of the exterior, while the innovative layout of the rooms on the first floor went on to start a trend.

■046 | St. Bartholomew's Hospital
City
James Gibbs, Philip Hardwick
The intervention made by Gibbs, a good example of baroque secular architecture, is the most outstanding element in this hospital, which was founded in the 12th century. The original complex consisted of four buildings set around a quadrangular courtyard, although the one on the southern side was replaced in the 1930s.

■047 | Treasury Building
Westminster
William Kent, John Soane, Charles Barry
The central volume – the only one completed by Kent – is marked by its Palladian elegance and thrusting verticality. In 1824 the Treasury's premises were enlarged by Soane, although his addition was replaced in 1844 by a construction designed by Barry in the early Victorian style.

■048 | West Towers, Westminster Abbey
Westminster
Nicholas Hawksmoor
This was the last element added to the Abbey of Westminster, as well as the last public work completed by Hawksmoor before his death. The towers, made of Portland stone, illustrate the resurgence of the Gothic style in the 18th century.

PLANNING THE NEW RESIDENTIAL NEIGHBOURHOODS

The 1774 Building Act regulated the appearance of new residential neighbourhoods, giving the go-ahead to not only the intensive development of Bloomsbury and Marylebone but also other districts further from central London, such as Hampstead, Dulwich, Highbury and Camden Town. The meticulous urban configuration called for streets, squares and crescents, along with a proliferation of the ubiquitous Georgian terrace house. Property developers, usually far removed from the world of architecture, were inspired by the new simplified versions of *Vitruvius Britannicus*, which made classical rules accessible to uninitiated speculators.

SIR WILLIAM CHAMBERS

The forerunner of the modern architect, Chambers (1726–1796) is known for his neoclassical designs, which come under the umbrella of late Palladianism. Somerset House ◼059 is the building that most faithfully reflects his classical output, although his work was also significantly marked by exoticism. He came back from his various journeys to India and China enamoured of Oriental art, and the principles he learned in Asia were applied to his buildings for Kew Gardens, including the Pagoda and the now long-gone Chinese Temple, Turkish Mosque and Arabian Alhambra.

A NEW RESIDENTIAL CONCEPT: THE TERRACE HOUSE

The need to accommodate London's growing population triggered the appearance of a type of residence that concentrated a large number of homes in a relatively small plot of land. Terrace houses, with their narrow façades largely built of brick, bestowed the desired architectural coherence on entire streets and squares. This new four-story residential format, with a rectangular floor space flanked by party walls that supported chimneys, marked the introduction of industrial production into domestic architecture, through elements such as iron railings and standard models of windows.

1745	1750	1752	1752	1754	1768

◼049 | Horse Guards
Westminster
William Kent, John Vardy
Vardy built this example of Palladian architecture from plans drawn up by Kent before his death. The ensemble of three buildings, arranged around a courtyard, once served as the front entrance to Buckingham Palace ◼068. Its unusual form is distinguished by the large Venetian windows with a frontispiece.

◼051 | Spencer House
Westminster
John Vardy
The outstanding feature of this residence, designed in a strict Palladian style, is its rear façade, which overlooks Green Park ●12. The dressed stone of the ground floor contrasts with the Tuscan columns on the upper storey that mark out the seven bays and support the frontispiece. The entrance hall contains a striking staircase with a tunnel arch resting on Ionic pillars.

◼053 | Dover House
Westminster
James Paine, Henry Holland
The private residence built by Paine, a follower of Palladio, in 1754, was hidden behind the new façade added by Holland in 1787. Holland's refurbishment stands out on account of the entrance hall endowed with a translucent vault, which filters sunlight and illuminates the marble columns and floor.

◼050 | Manresa House
Wandsworth
William Chambers
Manresa House, built for the Earl of Bessborough (who originally lent his name to the building), is one of the most authentic examples of Palladianism in England. This is clearly evident in the proportions of the Ionic portico, which are identical to those designed by Palladio in Vicenza.

◼052 | Mansion House
City
George Dance the Elder
The official residence of the Lord Mayor of London is a Palladian building, adorned on its main façade with an imposing portico that is raised above the bustle of the street by two flights of steps. Distinctive double-height attics emerge from behind the frontispiece, although the most attractive feature of Mansion House is its splendid interior.

◼054 | Adelphi
Westminster
James, William and Robert Adam
The groundbreaking Adelphi, of which only a few buildings remain, was developed and designed by the Adam brothers. A base made up of storage areas was intended to compensate for the slope of the land, while serving as a platform for a complex of 11 residential buildings, all decorated with exquisite elegance.

THE ADAM BROTHERS

The most enterprising trio of the 18th century was made up of three brothers: the architects Robert and James, supported by William, who looked after their financial matters. After mainly working outside London, the brothers decided to branch out as property developers by transforming a slum into a luxurious residential complex. Thus was born the Adelphi, of which little now remains. Its name ('brothers' in Greek) reflected the strong fraternal bonds linking the Adams. Their daring neoclassical style, impregnated with exotic and neo-Gothic influences, was criticised by the arbiters of architectural fashion but was admired by artists of the period.

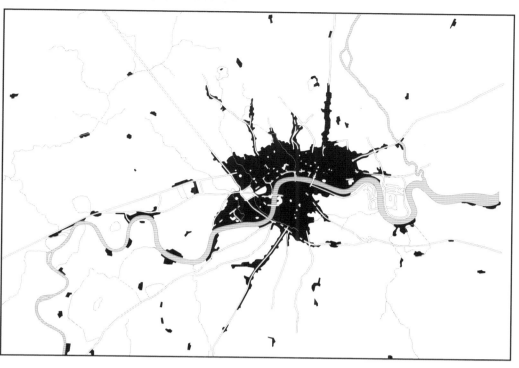

London in the 18th century

1770   1771   1774   1775   1776   1776

■056 | Apsley House
Westminster
Robert Adam, Benjamin and Philip Wyatt
In 1828 the Wyatts transformed this urban residence with exposed brickwork into a neoclassical mansion by cladding it with stone and adding a Corinthian portico on the west elevation. Adam's intervention is, however, still visible in the interior, which now plays host to the Wellington Museum.

■057 | Stone Buildings
Camden
Robert Taylor, Philip Hardwick
This splendid example of Palladianism, built entirely of Portland stone, boasts four storeys crowned by a cornice and a balustrade, organised around an inner courtyard. The west elevation, which faces Lincoln's Inn Gardens ●35, is distinguished by a stern austerity, in contrast to the Corinthian columns marking both its ends.

■059 | Somerset House
City
William Chambers, Robert Smirke, James Pennethorne
This complex set between the Strand and the river displays the same repetitive format as great urban residences like the Adelphi ■054 designed by the Adam brothers. Unlike the relatively modest elevation on the Strand, the extremely long façade reflects the imposing dimensions of the central courtyard.

■055 | Albany
Westminster
William Chambers, Henry Holland
The main entrance to this small urban mansion is on Piccadilly, which leads to the former Melbourne House. The other entrance, on Burlington Gardens, opens on to the courtyard where Holland built two parallel blocks in 1803, in response to a commission to turn the house into flats.

■058 | Royal Artillery Barracks
Greenwich
The impressive south façade of this old military residence extends from either side of a small triumphal arch in its centre. The two- and three-storey brick buildings are linked by white colonnades the height of the ground floor. The interiors have been totally refurbished, although the original dining room has remained intact.

■060 | Three Mills
Newham
The abundance of waterways in this area prompted the construction of several mills, including the Three Mills distillery, of which these buildings formed part. The oldest section dates back to 1776, while the slate domes next to the clock tower were built in 1813.

041 | St. Mary-le-Strand
James Gibbs

This church stands on an island amidst the London traffic. Its simple form, with a rectangular floor plan and seven bays long, is set off on the north and south elevations by two rows of openings, one of them blind. A balustrade decorated with urns crowns the perimeter of the building and frames the distinctive tower with three floors plus a pinnacle, now a landmark in the Strand although it did not feature in the original project. The semicircular portico on the western façade is inspired by Santa Maria della Pace, designed by the Mannerist Pietro da Cortona. Inside, the upper windows, topped by a Roman arch, are flanked by Corinthian columns. Both the nave and the apse are distinguished by the delicate finishing of their ceilings. Although the Italianate influence is apparent in this design drawn up by Gibbs, he later inclined towards a purer Palladianism (a style better appreciated by the Tory government that gave him work).

DISTRICT The City
LOCATION Strand, WC2
DATE OF CONSTRUCTION 1717

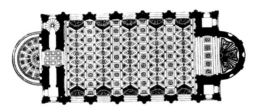

Soffits plan

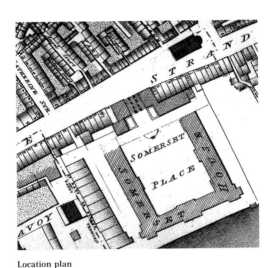

Location plan

Ground floor

West elevation

NEW AMENITIES FOR AN IMPERIAL CAPITAL

In the early 19th century, London was still deficient in many cultural, sanitary and infrastructural amenities. In the 1820s and 1830s, the city played host to the new democratic institutions that appeared after the tumultuous turn of the century. This was paralleled by an increase in the number of hospitals and cemeteries, as well as an expansion of cultural and leisure facilities, as exemplified by the opening of the British Museum ■067 and London Zoo. Transport and commerce were similarly enriched by the development of the railway network and the emergence of new markets, restaurants, banks, shopping arcades and hotels.

THE APOGEE OF THE NEO-GOTHIC

Romanticism brought with it an increased interest in the Middle Ages. By the second half of the 18th century, the writer Horace Walpole had already built his neo-Gothic castle on Strawberry Hill, while other architects, such as the Adam brothers, fused details from the elaborate medieval style with other influences. The competition to rebuild the old Westminster Palace, destroyed by fire in 1834, marked the consolidation of Victorian neo-Gothic. It was won by Barry and the young Pugin, a lover of Gothic art, with a project that was unequivocally neo-Gothic.

JOHN NASH

John Nash (1752–1835) is particularly known for his design for Regent's Park ● 19, considered the precedent of the 'garden city' that would come into fashion decades later. This visionary architect defined a style that would be reproduced throughout the 19th century. His work reveals a mixture of different influences, from classicism to Picturesquism, from Gothic to Oriental art. Outstanding amongst his London projects are the renovation of Buckingham Palace ■066, the planning of Trafalgar Square ● 21 and the homes on Carlton House Terrace ■067, completed just before his death.

1811   1814   1816   1819   1822   1823

■061 | Dulwich Gallery
Southwark
John Soane

This building, made to house an art collection donated to Dulwich College, was the first private art gallery to open in London. The design reflects Soane's later phase of neo-classical abstraction, and it is particularly famous for visual tricks created by its intricate brickwork.

■063 | Royal Opera Arcade
Westminster
John Nash, G. S. Repton

Only a few years after the invention of this type of building in Paris, Nash completed the Royal Opera House ● 83, complete with its own shopping gallery. Its shop windows, lit by means of glassed vaults, were installed only on the western façade, as the opposite side contained additional entrances to the opera house.

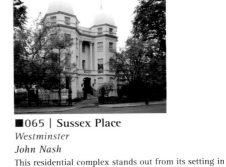

■065 | Sussex Place
Westminster
John Nash

This residential complex stands out from its setting in Regent's Park ● 19 on account of its unusual combination of architectural elements, inspired by the Brighton Pavilion. These origins are particularly evident in the octagonal domes, the central Corinthian domes and the polygonal windows of the gallery.

■062 | Stables of the Royal Hospital
Kensington
John Soane

This simple building alongside Wren's hospital demonstrates the main characteristics of Soane's style. The repetition of the arches and the simple pedestal of Portland stone comprise the only decorative elements on the brick façades.

■064 | St. Pancras
Camden
William Inwood

The pagan inspiration for this church caused a degree of controversy. The rectangular building followed the model of St. Martin-in-the-Fields ■044: an Ionic portico in front of an octagonal tower. The volumes added to the west are adorned with a row of caryatids, copied from the Erecteion in Athens.

■066 | St. Mary's, Wyndham Place
Westminster
Robert Smirke

This church dominates the neighbouring buildings on account of its splendid portico with Ionic columns and its slender tower topped with a cupola. The most striking feature of the main volume, with its exposed brickwork and square floor plan, is the Doric colonnade supporting the delicate coffered ceiling.

THE PRINCE REGENT AND REGENT'S PARK

The years of peace that followed the Battle of Waterloo (1815) coincided with the great architectural initiatives of the Prince Regent. Nash presented the future George IV with an ambitious plan for the old property of Marylebone Park that conformed with the urban developments of the 18th century while also establishing a precedent for the 'garden city'. Regent's Park ●19 was to contain several clusters of villas and stuccoed terrace houses, along with a large expanse of green containing botanical gardens and zoological parks, but various setbacks made it necessary to simplify the initial plan during the construction process.

THE URBANISATION OF LONDON IN THE VICTORIAN ERA

Queen Victoria, whose long reign stretched from 1837 to 1901, was considered by the expanding middle class as the incarnation of its ideals of sobriety and rectitude. The monarch's popularity was also enhanced by the economic boom of the 19th century, which favoured the prime movers of London's property development. Cubitt, the shrewdest speculator of the Victorian era, knew how to create a product to suit each social class: luxury residences for the aristocracy in Belgravia, terrace houses for the middle classes and professionals in Pimlico and Bloomsbury, and modest homes for the dock workers on the Isle of Dogs.

THE GREAT EXHIBITION (1851)

The Great Exhibition, promoted by Prince Albert, attracted six million visitors from all over the world eager to discover the latest advances in art and industry. Hyde Park ●13 was the setting chosen to install the venue for this momentous event: the Crystal Palace, a colossal metal-and-glass structure over 500 meters long and 120 meters wide. This exhibition, coinciding with a period of great optimism and confidence in the future, boosted the West End, Oxford Street and Knightsbridge as areas for shopping and entertainment, as well as generating enormous profits for its organisers.

1823   1825   1827   1827   1828   1828

■067 | British Museum
Camden
Robert Smirke

The State commissioned the neoclassical architect Robert Smirke to build a new public museum to house its abundant stock of art treasures. The project began with the magnificent 90-m-long (295-ft-long) library, while the portico and Ionic colonnade were added later, as was the vaulted reading room ▲50.

■069 | Carlton House Terrace
Westminster
John Nash

Just before his death in 1835, Nash completed this residential complex made up of two white stone volumes 140 m (459 ft) long, each resting on platforms facing the Mall ●15. The decoration on the robust Doric columns on the bases makes use of cast iron, which was a novelty at that time.

■071 | Covent Garden Market
Westminster
Charles Fowler

After playing host to a temporary market for over two hundred years, Jones' Covent Garden ●14 changed its appearance with the construction of a new permanent market, made up of a central gallery flanked by two large shopping malls, all covered with an iron-and-glass structure surrounded by an elegant granite colonnade.

■068 | Buckingham Palace
Westminster
John Nash, Edward Blore, Aston Webb

Nash was the first architect who was commissioned to turn Buckingham House into a royal palace. His west façade overlooking the garden has survived until today, while the remainder was refurbished by Blore in 1847 to increase the building's capacity. In the 20th century, the east façade was overhauled once again, in neoclassical style, by Webb ▲59.

■070 | University College London
Camden
William Wilkins, J. Gandy-Deering

The neoclassical architect William Wilkins endowed this new educational institution, the foundation stone of London University, with an imposing portico ten Doric columns wide that is backed by a dome. Four decades later, Hayter Lewis added the north and south wings, although their ends were not completed until the late 20th century.

■072 | Athenaeum
Westminster
Decimus Burton

A large portico of Doric columns marks the entrance to this building, one of the finest examples of neoclassicism in London. Pallas Athena presides over the first-floor balcony, complete with windows decorated with a blue and white frieze. The attic that rises up behind the balustrade was added in 1899.

CHARLES BARRY

A Londoner by birth, Barry (1795–1860) studied in Italy from 1817 to 1820, where he discovered the work of Renaissance masters that would have a lasting effect on his career. After travelling through Europe and Asia, he returned to England to design two of the clubs in Pall Mall, the Travellers Club ■073 and the Reform Club, the latter inspired by small Renaissance palaces. Although he was also responsible for the Treasury Building ■047 in Whitehall, Barry is above all famous for the large neo-Gothic Parliament complex in Westminster ■075, where he worked alongside Augustus Welby Pugin.

LIFE IN THE SLUMS

London's less fortunate citizens survived as best they could in the slums of the East End and parts of the West End, as described so graphically by Charles Dickens. The devastating outbreaks of cholera caused by overcrowding and insalubrious living conditions between the 1830s and the 1850s roused the previously indifferent government to take action and develop two complementary strategies for doing away with the slums. The first consisted of moving their inhabitants into state-subsidised homes and workhouses, while the second involved the demolition of sub-standard housing to open up new transport routes in their place.

THE DEVELOPMENT OF METROPOLITAN TRANSPORT

There was a spectacular development of the transport network in the 19th century. The city's main railway stations, Euston, St. Pancras ▲28, Victoria ▲25 and King's Cross ▲23, were all built between 1830 and 1870. The office workers and craftsmen who settled in the new residential suburbs that mushroomed after 1850 commuted to the centre by means of an extensive public transport system. New metropolitan train lines took advantage of bridges and tunnels crossing the Thames, which allowed the city's first underground train to be launched in 1863.

■ CHRONOLOGY

| 1829 | 1829 | 1835 | 1844 | 1867 | 1874 |

■073 | Travellers Club
Westminster
Charles Barry
This Renaissance-style neighbour to the Athenaeum ■072 stands on Pall Mall, an area that has been famous since the 19th century for its numerous gentlemen's clubs. The simple stucco façade of this two-storey building five bays wide is crowned by an attractive cornice.

■075 | Houses of Parliament
Westminster
Charles Barry, Augustus Welby Pugin
A year after Edward the Confessor's original palace was destroyed by a fire, the tandem of Barry and Pugin undertook the construction of this neo-Gothic complex bounded, to the north, by the tower of Big Ben and, to the south, by the Victoria Tower.

■077 | Royal Albert Hall
Westminster
Captain Francis Fowke
This extraordinary cylinder with a seating capacity of 8,000 rises amidst a striking collection of Victorian architecture. Its brick and terracotta structure, decorated with a frieze, is covered by a spectacular vault of glass and iron.

■074 | King's College
Westminster
Robert Smirke
This building backing on to Somerset House ■059 formed part of William Chambers' plan to renovate the skyline alongside the Thames. The complex's lack of originality attracted fierce criticism, especially in the light of the project drawn up by Smirke himself in the same period for the British Museum ▲50.

■076 | Palm House, Kew Gardens
Richmond upon Thames
Decimus Burton, Richard Turner
This innovative, curved structure made of iron and glass houses all the species of palm tree known to mankind. The building is notable for not only its lightness (despite its considerable dimensions) but also the complex intersections of its volumes.

■078 | Royal Courts of Justice
Westminster
George Edmund Street
The irregularly shaped main façade of this example of late neo-Gothic is distinguished by three elements: the clock tower, the entrances to the courtyard and the Great Hall, a spectacular room over 25 m (82 ft) high with a particularly strong Gothic inspiration.

CLEANING UP THE CITY

The propagation of the harmful effects of the insalubrious slums to all parts of the city prompted the creation, in 1859, of the Metropolitan Board of Works, which set about building a new sewage system. Similarly, the Victoria, Albert and Chelsea Embankments were constructed to accelerate the flow of the river and avoid the accumulation of pestilent sludge along its sides. In 1889, the London County Council (LCC), which replaced the Metropolitan Board of Works, intensified the fight against the slums and encouraged the construction of new houses and parks for the working classes.

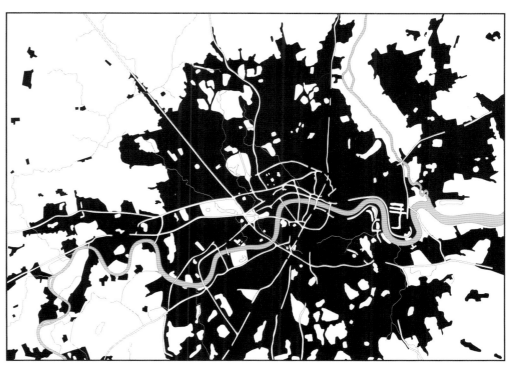

London in the 19th century

| 1876 | 1879 | 1879 | 1895 | 1897 | 1897 |

■079 | Swan House
Kensington
Richard Norman Shaw
This example of the return to the Queen-Anne style in domestic architecture stands out on account of its originality and elegance, largely based on the combination of different types of windows to mark the hierarchy of the storeys.

■081 | Royal Arcade
Westminster
This elegant, Victorian style shopping arcade, designed to link Brown's Hotel with Bond Street, is 40 m (131 ft) long, with nine shops on each side. The galleries – one for each shop – are separated by arches adorned with an open frontispiece that support the glass roof.

■083 | Tate Gallery
Westminster
Sidney Smith, Romaine Walker,
J. Russell Pope
The Tate Gallery, set on the grounds of an old prison, was enlarged over the course of the 20th century. The central dome and sculpture galleries were added in 1937, while the Clore Gallery, designed by Stirling and Wilford, was completed in 1985. Another notable addition from the same decade was the Whistler Restaurant.

■080 | Prudential Assurance
City
Alfred and Paul Waterhouse
The prosperity of the 19th-century insurance companies made possible the construction of this terracotta neo-Gothic palace, which was completed by Paul Waterhouse, Alfred's son, in the early years of the 20th century. The symmetrical main façade sports several rows of windows with a pointed arch.

■082 | Mary Ward Settlement
Camden
Smith and Brewer
Despite the clear influences of Mackintosh, Townsend and Shaw, this building offers a distinctive and original interpretation of the Arts and Crafts idiom. Symmetry disappears next to the main entrance, while the diagonal windows above the auxiliary entrances create a novel effect.

■084 | Whitechapel Art Gallery
Tower Hamlets
C. H. Townsend
Townsend, one of the main exponents of the Arts and Crafts style, was responsible for this innovative and imposing art gallery. The main elevation is distinguished by a portico that is set back asymmetrically from a storey with no other openings. Also striking are the two square towers on either side of the building. ▲83

■075 | Houses of Parliament
Charles Barry, Augustus Welby Pugin

Barry undertook the design of the building's symmetrical composition, while Pugin was responsible for the exuberant neo-Gothic details, most notably the sculptures and the delicate ornamentation with wood and carved stone. Although the main sections were already in use in 1852, Big Ben and the Victoria Tower were not completed until 1858 and 1860, respectively. A central north-south axis articulates the buildings, arranged in a configuration that reflects the British parliamentary system, with the Commons and the Lords, as well as halls reserved for the use of the monarchy. The entrance opens on to the large octagonal foyer, which leads in its turn to the Commons Chamber, to the left, and the House of Lords, to the right. The former was rebuilt by Giles Gilbert Scott after World War II, while the latter features Pugin's most accomplished work in London.

DISTRICT Westminster
LOCATION House of Commons, SW1
MAXIMUM HEIGHT 90 m (295 ft)
DATE OF CONSTRUCTION 1835

Detail of the clock

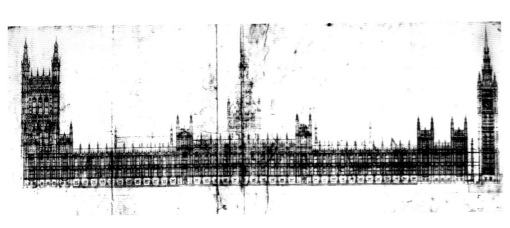

South elevation

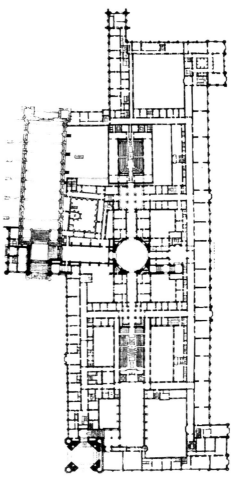

Ground plan

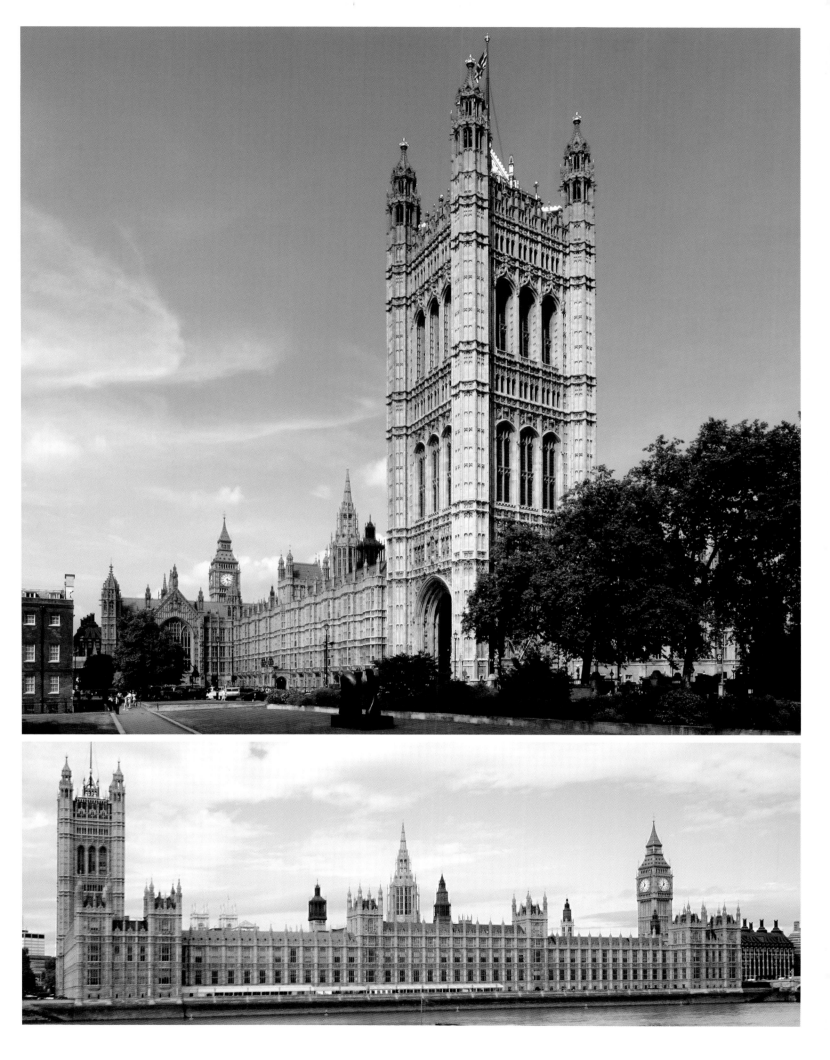

ARCHITECTURE AND THE ARTS AND CRAFTS MOVEMENT

William Morris reacted to the excesses of 19th-century industrialisation by founding the Arts and Crafts Movement in 1888. This was paralleled in architecture by the Eclectic movement, headed by Shaw, Webb and Ashbee; its domestic architecture, described by the German writer Hermann Muthesius in *Das Englische Haus* (1904), penetrated the domain of public buildings in the early 20th century. Morris' socialist philosophy combined with Webb and Lethaby's architectural ideas to pave the way for the new housing programmes promoted by the LCC's Architecture Department, one of the greatest achievements of the Arts and Crafts Movement in England.

THE CITY ADAPTS TO THE NEW SOCIETY

The outlying neighbourhoods constituted the basis for London's suburban expansion until the 1930s. These new estates of family houses were made possible by the development of the Underground, and the latter's corporate image brought a sense of unity and common identity to London's great conurbation. The popularisation of the motor car between the two world wars also sparked the construction of numerous roads around the city. Social changes, such as the massive incorporation of middle-class women into the workforce, were also reflected in domestic architecture, which was characterised by the growing construction of blocks of flats.

ILLUSTRIOUS IMMIGRANTS IN THE INTERWAR PERIOD

Before the outbreak of World War II, many prestigious architects and artists sought refuge in London from the totalitarianism on the Continent, including Mendelsohn, Gropius, Lubetkin, Moholy-Nagy and Breuer. They brought with them new architectural ideas that crashed against the prevailing neo-Georgian style, and their enthusiasm inspired a new generation of British architects, particularly Maxwell Fry, Jane Drew, Francis Skinner and Denys Lasdun. The main exponent of modern pre-war architecture was Lubetkin, with his Tecton studio, which was responsible for the London Zoo and the Highpoint residential blocks.

28

■ CHRONOLOGY

1901	1904	1906	1907	1908	1920

■085 | Harrods
Kensington
Stevens and Munt
The Edwardian splendour of this department store, modelled on La Samaritaine in Paris, occupies an entire block, with nearly 14 acres of shopping space spread over its five floors. The exterior, which is clad with terracotta tiles, is embellished with detailed decoration, while its interior contains superb Art-Deco features.

■086 | Barkers
Kensington
Bernard George
George completed the project that William Barker had set in motion over 30 years earlier. Its Art-Deco façade, along with that of the neighbouring Derry and Toms, is yet another example of the importation of architectural styles from the Continent in the interwar period.

■087| Admiralty Arch
Westminster
Aston Webb
This Portland-stone structure facing Buckingham Palace ■068 from the far end of the Mall ●15 forms part of the route between the royal residence and St. Paul's Cathedral ■028. The Corinthian order is complemented by Edwardian ornamental motifs, particularly noticeable on the upper level.

■088 | Selfridges
Westminster
R. F. Atkinson, Daniel Burnham
Like Harrods ■085, this department store occupies an entire block. A sturdy, profusely decorated Ionic colonnade stands on the base of the ground floor to guard the three intermediate floors, which are hidden behind metal panels.

■089 | Royal Automobile Club
Westminster
Mewès and Davis, with E. Keynes
The RAC was one of the various clubs that were founded to celebrate the arrival of the motor car in the cosmopolitan London of Edward VII. The modern steel-and-concrete structure of this imposing building clad with Portland stone made it possible to take advantage of the basement to install, among other amenities, a sunken marble swimming pool.

■090 | Westmorald House
Westminster
John Burnet, Thomas Tait
This project formed part of Nash's renovation of Regent Street, which was resumed after World War I. Using a device that recurred in other buildings by Burnet, the classically styled façades meet each other at rounded vertices. These are decorated with columns and crowned with a dome clad with copper.

LONDON DURING WORLD WAR II

The onslaught of the German air force in World War II brought severe physical and psychological damage on a city that had not been directly attacked since the 11th century. The Blitz of 1940 and subsequent bombardments obliterated the docks and the East End, as well as causing considerable devastation in the City. The bombs destroyed 20 churches, numerous trade-union headquarters and two of the Inns of Court, the Temple ●01 and Gray's Inn ■020. Nearly one million Londoners were evacuated to rural areas during the course of the war, but the air attacks still left more than 20,000 victims.

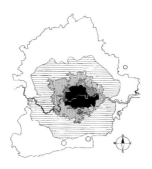

RECONSTRUCTION PLANS

The reconstruction process threw up several thorny problems, as it represented a chance to do away with the slums and modernise certain urban areas. In 1943 Abercrombie and Forshaw were already presenting their plans for the county of London, while the former put forward his Greater London Region Plan a year later. In 1946 Holden and Holford presented the City of London Plan, and that same year saw the passing of the New Towns Act, which anticipated the construction of new satellite towns like Harlow and Stevenage, designed to rehouse the thousands of Londoners who had lost their homes.

THE NEW STARS OF THE LONDON SKYLINE

In the early 1950s, the LCC continued in the forefront of residential architecture with its new programmes for the East End, South London and Roehampton. Despite its good intentions, based on the principles of Le Corbusier and Swedish public housing policies, the domestic architecture of this era is generally marked by its poor quality and lack of coherence. By the 1960s, the city's skyline had become a forest of towers in which it was impossible to distinguish the soaring hotels and office buildings from the LCC's blocks of flats.

1924   1929   1930   1932   1932   1934

■091 | Britannic House
City
Edwin Lutyens, Peter Inskip, Peter Jenkins Architects
Edwin Lutyens, Peter Inskip, Peter Jenkins Architects This building's impressive concave façade echoes the oval shape of Finsbury Circus. The top three of the seven storeys are decorated with Corinthian pillars that flank the large windows. A recent refurbishment resulted in a semicircular inner courtyard with a glass roof, designed to take full advantage of natural light.

■092 | Battersea Power Station
Wandsworth
Halliday and Agate, Giles Gilbert Scott, S. L. Pearce
The construction of this building with a distinctive silhouette was completed in 1953. The four 113-m-high (370-ft-high) chimneys dominate the Art-Deco interior, which contrasts with the industrial setting around it. There are plans to convert this landmark on the south bank of the Thames into a multipurpose complex.

■093 | Royal Masonic Hospital
Hammersmith and Fulham
John Burnet, Tait and Lorne
This big redbrick hospital with a symmetrical composition was Burnet's last project. It is inspired by the architects Willem Marinus Dudok – for his skill in handling large volumes and using brickwork for providing detail – and Erich Mendelsohn – the source of the sharply curved terraces.

■094 | Broadcasting House
Westminster
Val Myers and Watson-Hart
This monolithic symbol of the increasing importance of radio in the 1930s and 1940s displays Georgian proportions on the openings to match the architecture of the neighbouring buildings. The building's curved façade, which reflects the dimensions of its plot, thrusts outward like the bow of a ship.

■095 | Daily Express
City
Ellis Clarke and Atkinson, Owen Williams
This glass-clad steel structure with curved arrises, standing in the mythical heart of London's journalism, was the epitome of new architecture in its day. The entrance lobby constitutes a magnificent example of Art-Deco interior design, with extravagant ornamental reliefs and atmospheric lighting.

■096 | Senate House
Camden
Charles Holden
This robust tower block, built as the administrative centre for the University of London, represents a very pure form of neoclassicism, as evidenced by its austere façades of Portland stone. The versatility of the interiors is ideally suited to the multiple functions of the buildings.

FESTIVAL OF BRITAIN

The launching of London's reconstruction was marked by the Festival of Britain, which took place in 1951, a century after the extremely successful Great Exhibition. The government organised this event to celebrate the country's recovery after the harsh years that followed the war. The chosen venue was Lambeth, on the south side of the river. After demolishing what was left of its old buildings, several temporary structures were put up around the only permanent construction, the Royal Festival Hall ■102. This great concert hall has since been joined by various other cultural institutions, which have completely transformed the South Bank ●65 in just a few decades.

ELIZABETH II

The coronation of Elizabeth II (b. 1926) in 1952 represented a confirmation of the recovery phase that the country had now entered, after the impetus of the Festival of Britain in the previous year. In over five decades on the throne, Elizabeth II has embodied the modernization of the institution she represents, making it more accessible to the population while also shunning the excessive intrusion of the media. Her notable awareness of British political life has been complemented by her continuation of the pageantry expected of the monarchy, in particular the elaborate celebrations commemorating the first 25 and 50 years of her reign.

THE SEARCH FOR NEW RESIDENTIAL MODELS

The post-war public initiative to alleviate the shortage of housing by building blocks of flats was fiercely questioned in the 1960s. The collapse of Ronan Point raised many doubts about the suitability of large concrete blocks that were often put up too quickly on a shoestring budget. This accident not only triggered residential programmes on a more human scale, such as Lillington Gardens (1972) in Belgravia, but also instilled in British society a certain distrust of modern architecture, represented in the popular imagination by skyscrapers.

■ CHRONOLOGY

1934   1934   1935   1935   1936   1939

■097 | Pioneer Health Centre
Southwark
Owen Williams
This centre for preventive medicine follows the industrial model of other projects by Williams, who created a large central area given over to the swimming pool, separated from other secondary spaces by translucent screens. The glass façades with their exposed structure were renovated by LCC Architects in 1954.

■098 | Penguin Pool
Westminster
Berthold Lubetkin and Tecton
This pool was the fruit of the architects' behaviourist research, which led them to design a space intended to stimulate its occupants. The various flooring materials applied to the reinforced-concrete base aimed to provoke a reaction from the penguins, while the narrow curved ramps put their sense of balance to the test.

■099 | Simpson's
Westminster
Joseph Emberton
Unlike other department stores of the period, this pioneering design, with its austere rows of horizontal openings and its projection on the top floor, drew on the modern architecture of the Continent. Its spacious interior, organised as a sequence of rooms, is enhanced by the opulence of the materials used.

■100 | Reuters and Press Association
City
Edwin Luytens, Smee and Houchin
The L-shape ground plan of this building frames the beautiful St. Bride's Church designed by Wren. The windows, made with a steel structure clad with Portland stone, grow gradually narrower towards the top. The uppermost floor is crowned by an independent concave volume.

■101 | Peter Jones
Kensington
W. Crabtree
This department store displays one of the period's most outstanding façades of curtain walling. Its curved elevation is adapted to the building's awkward placement on the corner of a square, while the window displays on the ground floor reduce the passerby's perception of the overall dimensions at street level.

■102 | Greenwich Council
Greenwich
Culpin and Bowers
This brick building's balanced composition of vertical and horizontal lines is inspired by the legacy of the Dutch architect Willem Marinus Dudok. Its heterogeneous volumes culminate in a distinctive tower that allows this public building to be recognised from afar.

THE PUBLIC MAKES ITS VIEWS FELT

Architecture has gradually moved closer to the citizen and vice versa. The increased prominence of this discipline in the media and the population's higher level of education have encouraged members of the public to speak out and organize themselves, in the belief that they can make a difference. So, in the 1960s it was local action groups that put a stop to the carefree expansion of the railway network, which would have involved the disappearance of extensive areas of woodland close to London. Similarly, plans to renovate Covent Garden were also modified in the 1970s in response to the indignation of the local population.

London in the 20th century

1951   1955   1959   1962   1962   1963

■ 103 | **Royal Festival Hall**
Lambeth
LCC Architects Department, R. Matthew,
J. L. Martin, E. Williams and P. Moro
This concert hall, built for the Festival of Britain in 1951, served to introduce Londoners to modern architecture. The glass-and-concrete elevations make it possible to discern the imaginative layout of the foyers and staircases, as well as the forest of pillars that supports the concert hall.

■ 104 | **Bankside Power Station**
Southwark
Giles Gilbert Scott, Herzog and de Meuron
This old power station, readily identified by its distinguished tower, was converted into the Tate Modern ▲ 49 in 2000. Herzog and de Meuron respected the building's original structure, while adding a glass penthouse that lights up the huge turbine hall, now used as the entrance lobby.

■ 105 | **Barbican Estate**
City
Chamberlin, Powell and Bon
The post-war Labour government decided to build a new residential neighbourhood in a part of the City that had been devastated by bombs. The complex, which provides accommodation for 6,500 people, is made up of various types of buildings, from 125-m (410-ft) tower blocks to family houses, arranged around communal green spaces. ● 8

■ 106 | **New Scotland Yard**
Westminster
Chapman Taylor Partners
These two granite-and-glass buildings, standing on a triangular plot, were occupied by the police force when it outgrew the headquarters designed by Shaw on the Embankment. The block closest to the street, which contains shops on the ground floor, is distinguished by the rationalism of its composition.

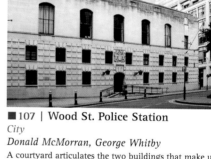

■ 107 | **Wood St. Police Station**
City
Donald McMorran, George Whitby
A courtyard articulates the two buildings that make up this imposing complex: one is square and three storeys high, the other has twelve floors. Although the result represented a return to the classicism of Lutyens, specific features on the façades situate the composition in the period following the Festival of Britain.

■ 108 | **London Telecom Tower**
Camden
Architecture Department of the Ministry of Public Works
This cylinder made of concrete, steel and glass is considered an exceptional feat of engineering. Apart from the open section bearing aerials, the 175-m high (574-ft-high) tower is clad with a curtain wall that protects the offices on the storeys inside.

■ 104 | Bankside Power Station | Tate Modern

Herzog and De Meuron

The factors that favoured the conversion of this old power station into a museum included the huge amount of space available and the riverside location opposite the City. The latter feature was highlighted by the construction of a pedestrian bridge connecting it with the City, and in addition a boat link has been established with the other Tate building on the north bank. As regards the building itself, the architects came up with a project that sought to preserve the essential character of the old power station, which originally consisted of a large turbine hall, 35 m (115 ft) high and 152 m (499 ft) long, that adjoined a boiler house. The former was used to house the enormous entrance lobby, while the latter contains the galleries, spread over three storeys around the central staircases. A two-floor glass penthouse was added to the original roof, providing panoramic views of the surrounding area.

DISTRICT Southwark
LOCATION Bankside, SE1
SURFACE AREA 76,400 sq. m
DATE OF CONSTRUCTION 2000

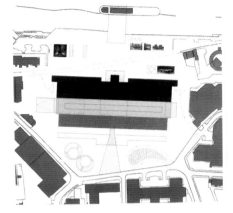

Location plan

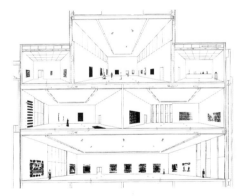

Section in perspective

Axonometric view

Ground plan

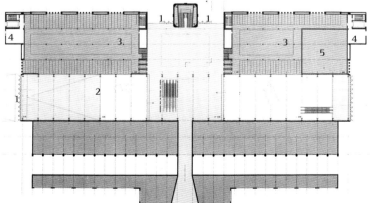

1- Entrances
2- Turbine hall
3- Galleries
4- Service entrance
5- Storage area

Cross-section

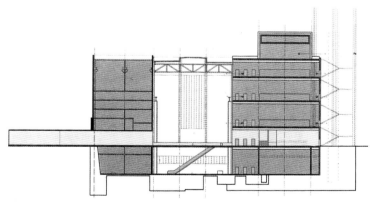

LOST OPPORTUNITIES IN CENTURIES-OLD NEIGHBOURHOODS

The closure of the docks in the 1970s left a large area available for new urban projects. Unfortunately, both the docklands and the City suffered from the property boom of the 1980s, when thousands of square feet of office space were built with barely any overall planning, along with luxury housing for the employees of the new companies that set up shop in the area. Although few buildings stand out for their architectural value, this conglomeration of volumes with granite-clad steel or concrete structures does constitute a socio-economic and architectural phenomenon in its own right.

ABOLITION OF THE GREATER LONDON COUNCIL

The Greater London Council (GLC) closed its doors in 1986. Its abolition formed part of a series of privatisations undertaken by the Conservative government in the 1980s. The GLC, a brainchild of the Labour Party, was replaced by numerous small bodies with specific but diverse interests, which resulted in an evident lack of coordination and an inability to satisfy the city's basic infrastructural needs. The Conservatives' policies also slashed investment in public housing, at the same time as the construction boom was filling the City and the docklands with office blocks.

RICHARD ROGERS

Richard Rogers (b. 1933) is particularly well known for his key role in founding the architectural movement known as High Tech. After winning the competition for the Pompidou Centre in 1971, he formed his own company. His projects are characterised by his passion for technology and his commitment to sustainability and the rejuvenating power of urban development. His projects in London include the HQs of Lloyd's ■114, Reuters and Channel 4 ■125, and, more recently, the Millennium Dome ■129, Terminal 5 at Heathrow Airport and the new office areas of Canary Wharf ●54 and Paddington Basin.

■ CHRONOLOGY

| 1964 | 1964 | 1967 | 1970 | 1977 | 1978 |

■109 | Queen Elizabeth Hall, Purcell Room and Hayward Gallery
Lambeth
LCC/GLC Architects Department; Hugh Bennett and Jack Whittle
These three buildings ▲46, along with the Royal Festival Hall ▲102, comprise the South Bank Centre ▲65. Planned along the lines of a city with different levels, these concrete volumes with serviceable roof terraces are linked by a number of bridges, allowing visitors to walk round the entire cultural complex.

■110 | The Economist
Westminster
Alison and Peter Smithson
These three towers of various heights contain the headquarters of *The Economist* and other offices and flats. This ensemble of concrete and Portland stone, next to St. James's Street, has succeeded in creating circulation areas in the vicinity and establishing an attractive contrast with the 18th-century architecture around it.

■111| Royal National Theatre
Lambeth
Denys Lasdun and Partners
The first performance by the National Theatre – an institution whose existence had been the subject of campaigns by intellectuals since the 19th century – took place in 1976. The building contains three auditoriums designed to stage both classical and experimental works. The building's various horizontal platforms serve as terraces with a view over the river. ▲87

■112 | College of Engineering and Science
Westminster
Lyons Israel and Ellis
In contrast with the 18th-century architecture around it, this eclectic group of forms is the sum total of diverse influences. The striking forms of the towers that contain the offices and laboratories are separated from the service areas.

■113 | Danish Embassy
Kensington
Arne Jacobsen, Dissing and Weitling
In the only project realised in London by this famous Danish architect, the elements that make up the building were designed individually. The façade on Sloane Street provides four storeys of offices protected by aluminium panels, plus a further two floors with both offices and flats.

■114 | Lloyd's of London
City
Richard Rogers Partnership
This steel sculpture, which has attracted both praise and criticism, was built on the site of the venerable insurance company's old neoclassical headquarters. The design undermines conventional notions of interior layout by placing the service areas on the façade, making it possible to set a spectacular 12-storey patio in the heart of the rectangular floor plan.

MODERNITY OR TRADITION?

Vision of Britain, published by the Prince of Wales in the late 1980s, invited the architectural community to consider the options of returning to traditional Palladianism or losing themselves in an undecipherable future. The reduction of the debate to the concepts of classicism and modernity were fiercely criticised by numerous commentators and official bodies, including the Royal Institute of British Architects (RIBA). Even so, London's metropolitan area does indeed bear the signs of architectural blunders perpetrated by extremists in both the traditionalist and progressive camps, who emerged from the controversy in a stronger position.

MILLENNIUM COMMISSION

The creation of the National Lottery in 1994 created great expectations as its earnings would be donated to various non-profit making organizations, including the Millennium Commission. This body was founded with a built-in expiry date and a very specific aim: to raise funds to finance initiatives that celebrated the change of millennium. It invested over a million pounds in helping to bring to fruition almost 215 projects, 32 of them in London's metropolitan area. Of these, some of the most outstanding were the Mile End Park, the refurbishment of Southwark Cathedral ■003, the Tate Modern ■104 and the Great Court ▲50 of the British Museum ■065.

SIR NORMAN FOSTER

After studying architecture in Manchester and Yale, in 1967 this British architect founded Foster Associates, later to become Foster and Partners. Foster (b. 1935) is convinced that architecture is a form of public art and argues that every project should adapt to the culture and climate of the place in which it is set. He has succeeded in refuting much of the received wisdom attached to his discipline by focusing on each new problem in a fresh and original manner. He was awarded the Pritzker Prize in 1999. His most notable works in London include the Riverside complex, the City Hall ■130, the Canary Wharf station ■127 and 30 St. Mary Axe ■132.

1981   1987   1988   1988   1989   1989

■115 | National Westminster Tower
City
Richard Seifert and Partners
The concrete core of this building (known since 1995 as Tower 42) supports three projecting, asymmetrically arranged volumes. The surrounding steel columns protect the inset windows, which emphasise the verticality of this 183-m-high (600-ft-high) building with a cross section that reproduces the logo of the NatWest.

■117 | Sainsbury's
Camden
Nicholas Grimshaw and Partners
The supermarket, set in the flexible central space with a vaulted roof, forms part of a bigger project that also includes homes, workshops and a crèche. The exposed steel structure provides an industrial look and reveals the workings of the intricate engineering that holds up the complex.

■119 | Vogan's Mill
Southwark
Michael Squire Associates
The renovation of this port complex formed part of the transformation of the docks set in motion in the 1980s. The modernity of this slender 17-storey tower block, built on the site of an old grain silo, contrasts with the original façades of the warehouses, which have been converted into luxury housing.

■116 | Embankment Place
Westminster
Terry Farrell and Company
This enormous project, characterised by the coherence of its design, transformed Charing Cross Station and the surrounding area. The intervention opened up pedestrian precincts and created more than 32,000 sq. m of office space, situated in the volume raised above the tracks, flanked by four towers with service areas.

■118 | The Ark
Hammersmith and Fulham
Ralph Erskine
The inhospitable surroundings of this building cannot be seen from the interior, where ecological considerations have led to the isolation of the 15,000 sq. m of office space. The insulation of the steel structure on north façade is offset on the south side, where sunlight penetrates through a large central patio.

■120 | Reuters
Tower Hamlets
Richard Rogers and Partners
The main façade displays three distinct elements: the robust block of tinted glass provides the required privacy; the transparent volume reveals the company's human dimension and, finally, the exposed structure of the upper floors emphasizes the functional aspects of the building.

THE DOCKS TAKE ON A LEADING ROLE ONCE AGAIN

The property crisis at the start of the 1990s brought to a halt the incipient renovation of the docks that had started with One Canada Square. However, the subsequent economic recovery, along with the government's backing of the Jubilee Underground line, made it possible to resume the project for Canary Wharf ●54, which now serves as the headquarters of the main banks and media companies. This transformation, complemented by the installation of the Docklands Light Railway to Woolwich and Stratford, will culminate with the construction in the latter area of the buildings designed to host the Olympic Games in 2012.

THE RETURN OF THE SKYSCRAPER

In the early years of the 21st century there has been a noticeable trend towards a resumption of the skyward construction of the 1980s, and this has breathed new life into a controversy that appeared to have cooled in the 1990s. Some commentators argue that the offices on offer exceed the demand, but nevertheless there are at present, throughout the city, a substantial number of projects for skyscrapers with a completion date of around 2010, such as Renzo Piano's London Bridge Tower, Richard Rogers' Leadenhall Street block and the Vauxhall Tower, a 50-floor residential block designed by Broadway Malyan.

LONDON 2012: A NEW CHALLENGE

The 500-acre Olympic Park, situated alongside the River Lea in Stratford, is the undisputable star of the 2012 Olympic and Paralympic Games. The Park will provide East London with a new stadium and various sports complexes that will become public facilities for the new occupants of the Olympic Village once the games are over. The event will also serve to expand and modernize the transport network, with the continuation of the Docklands Light Railway to the east and the extension of the Channel Tunnel Rail Link, which will make it possible to travel by train from the city centre to the Continent in a mere two hours.

■ CHRONOLOGY

1990　　　　1991　　　　1991　　　　1992　　　　1994　　　　1998

■ 121 | **Riverside**
Wandsworth
Foster and Partners
This simple concrete-and-glass structure stands in an old industrial area between Battersea Bridge and Albert Bridge. When seen from the other side of the river, the glass façade reveals that the first two floors contain open-plan offices, while the remaining six are devoted to residential use.

■ 122 |
Tower Hamlets
Cesar Pelli and Associates,
Adamson Associates, Frederick Gibberd,
Coombes and Partners
This tower block has become a landmark, as its height of 244 m (800 ft) raises it above the rest of the area. Although its proportions are somewhat cumbersome, the repetitive, stripped-down format of the façade contrasts with the more elaborate buildings around it.

■ 123 | **Waterloo International Terminal**
Lambeth
Nicholas Grimshaw and Partners
Grimshaw built a light, steel-and-glass structure to protect the 400-m-long (1,312-ft-long) platforms, in homage to the complex iron roofs of the stations of the 19th century. In the basement, a reinforced-concrete box serves as a base for the two-storey viaduct that supports the tracks.

■ 124 | **Ludgate**
City
Skidmore, Owings and Merrill
The tight budgets of the 1990s led to a reduction in the ornamental elements on this building. The steel structure, arranged around a central square, stands on a configuration of springs that absorbs the vibrations emanating from the Underground.

■ 125 | **Channel 4**
Westminster
Richard Rogers and Partners
This HQ for a television company is set on the north and west sides of a square (the other sides are lined by housing blocks). The spectacular entrance on the northwest vertex leads to a complex where the contrast in its component elements alleviates the monumental effect.

■ 126 | **Thames Court**
City
Kohn Pedersen Fox
This five-storey building offers a panoramic view of the river from its south façade, which is clad in glass to reduce its visual impact. The main entrance on the north elevation, framed in stone, isolates the building from the heavy traffic, while the magnificent central courtyard illuminates the lower storeys.

WHERE IS THE CITY HEADING?

Canary Wharf is just the first stage in the eastward expansion that will characterize the 21st century. New neighbourhoods with varied functions will spread toward the Thames on what is known as the Thames Gateway, a former industrial belt, 60 km (37 mi) long, which is now very dilapidated and largely lacking in basic infrastructures. This initiative, viewed with suspicion by some ecological organisations, is intended to silence those critical voices that prophesise a return to the days of Dickens, with one London reserved for a privileged elite and another for the poor.

| 1999 | 1999 | 2001 | 2002 | 2002 | 2004 |

■ 127 | Canary Wharf Station
Tower Hamlets
Foster and Partners

The three glass canopies that identify the entrances to this addition to the Jubilee Line allows natural light to penetrate into the underground lobby and enables users to find their way more easily in the large central space, where the predominant materials are concrete, steel and glass.

■ 129 | Millennium Dome
Greenwich
Richard Rogers Partnership

This dome 320 m (1,050 ft) in diameter, an example of Rogers' high-tech architecture, covers a space flooded with light spanning over 100,000 sq. m. Over 70 km of steel cables hold up the glass-fibre roof covered with Teflon, supported by 12 masts 30 m (100 ft) high.

■ 131 | Laban Dance Centre
Lewisham
Herzog and de Meuron

In the post-industrial landscape of the docks, this semi-transparent parallelepiped covered with multi-coloured layers of plastic contains 13 dance studios, a theatre, a library and a café. The concave main façade leads to an interior with abundant bright spaces distinguished throughout by the presence of work by the Irish artist Michael Craig-Martin.

■ 128 | London Eye
Lambeth
Marks Barfield Architects

This 135-m-high Ferris wheel has become the city's foremost tourist attraction. The steel structure, similar in form to a bicycle wheel, supports 32 cabins with a bird's eye view that rise above the totally renovated park on the south bank of the river.

■ 130 | City Hall
Southwark
Foster and Partners

The volumes of this glass building were designed on the basis of a sphere modified by computer. It leans southward to maximise its energy efficiency, while its transparency symbolises the democratic process and invites visitors to go up to its terrace roof with panoramic views.

■ 132 | 30 St. Mary Axe
City
Foster and Partners

This revolutionary conical building looms above the densely packed tower blocks of the City. Its 41 storeys, crowned by a glass dome, house more than 75,000 sq. m of office and shopping space, reached by the new square that has been created around the building.

132 | 30 St. Mary Axe
Foster and Partners

This building, based on a radial floor plan, widens as it rises from the ground and then narrows on its upper storeys. This shape prevents it from becoming overpowering and makes full use of the space available inside, as well as offering less resistance to the wind and facilitating natural ventilation. The building is framed by a solid perimeter structure that made it possible to both extend the glass cladding over the entire façade and dispense with pillars on the storeys, which are connected vertically by courtyards. These not only function as meeting places but also distribute the air that passes through the panels on the façade, which can be opened. This building, which won the RIBA's Stirling Prize in 2004, is notable for its energy efficiency and its desire to humanise the workplace, as well as its respect for its urban context.

DISTRICT The City
LOCATION 30 St. Mary Axe, EC3
TOTAL HEIGHT 80 m (262 ft)
DATE OF CONSTRUCTION 2004

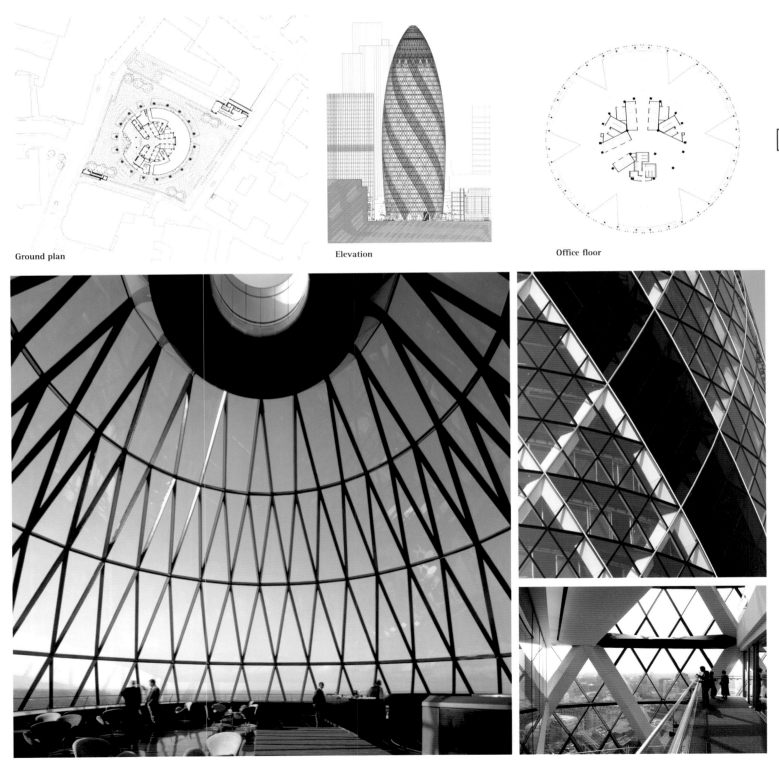

Ground plan

Elevation

Office floor

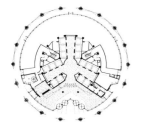

Office floor

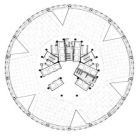

Fourth floor

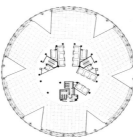

Seventh floor

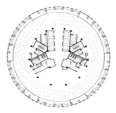

Ninth floor

Twentieth floor

Thirtieth floor

N

City

Westminster

Kensington and Chelsea | Hammersmith and Fulham

Camden | Islington | Hackney

Tower Hamlets | Newham | Greenwich | Lewisham

Southwark | Lambeth | Wandsworth

Outer West London
Brent, Ealing, Harrow, Hillingdon, Hounslow, Richmond upon Thames

Outer North London
Barnet, Enfield, Haringey, Redbridge, Waltham Forest

Outer East London
Barking and Dagenham, Bexley, Havering

Outer South London
Bromley, Croydon, Kingston upon Thames, Merton, Sutton

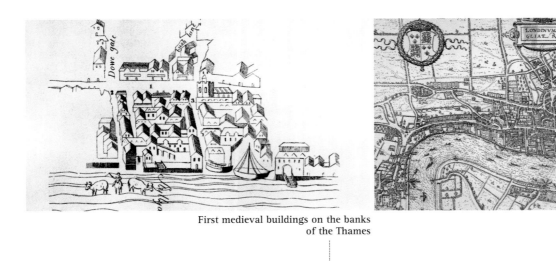

First medieval buildings on the banks
of the Thames

Map of the city

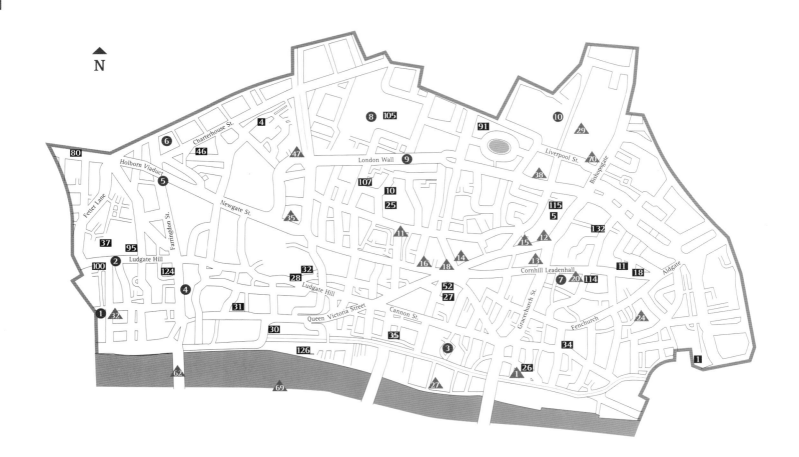

N

Charterhouse St.

80

Holborn Viaduct

6

46

47

London Wall

8 105

91

10

29

Liverpool St.

70

Bishopsgate

38

Fetter Lane

Farringdon St.

5

Newgate St.

107

35

10

25

115

5

1 32

37

95

Ludgate Hill

11

15 12

13

100 2

124

16 18 14

Cornhill Leadenhall

7 20 114

11 18

Aldgate

4

32

28

Ludgate Hill

52

27

31

Queen Victoria Street

Cannon St.

Gracechurch St.

24

Fenchurch

30

35

34

126

3

62

69

27

1 26

1

City

This borough spanning 3 sq. km (1⅕ sq. mi), bounded by Blackfriars ▲062 and Tower Bridge ▲064, has gradually been losing its population, although in the last few decades its residents have increased in number to reach the present level of 8,000. Despite the havoc wreaked by the Great Fire of 1666 and the wartime Blitz, the City has preserved the capital's oldest architectural remains, such as the Roman wall and the maze marked out by the medieval streets. A growing number of skyscrapers are now overshadowing the emblematic St. Paul's Cathedral ■020, which struggles to assert its time-honoured dominance.

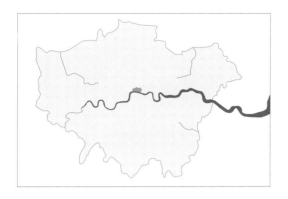

●1

●1 | THE TEMPLE
1350

This harmonious complex, which was largely rebuilt after the Blitz, comprises several buildings that were put up between the 12th and 20th centuries around a series of courtyards and gardens. By the 12th century, the Knights Templar had already installed themselves on these grounds, but after their dissolution in 1312 the complex was ceded to the Order of Saint John. This institution, in its turn, rented part of the property to the Inns of Court, which was finally granted ownership by James I in 1608. The members of the Middle and Inner Temple gradually replaced some of the original buildings with others better suited to their function, but those that remain include the round temple of the Knights Templar and the hall in the Middle Temple.

●2 | FLEET STREET
1520

This street, bounded to the west by Temple Bar and to the east by Ludgate Circus, owes its name to the nearby river that flowed into the Thames. Its western and eastern ends are marked by the churches of St. Dunstan and St. Bride, heralding the maze of alleyways that run off the main street. The Temple complex ●1 occupies much of the southern side, while the emblematic buildings that witnessed centuries of journalism still dot the street, although they are now far removed from the frenzied activity of the press. Since the 1990s, the former headquarters of newspapers have gradually been taken over by other businesses after the media companies moved camp to Canary Wharf ●54. This process culminated with the departure of Reuters in 2005.

●2

Panoramic view of the city in the reign of Elizabeth I

42

●3 | HOUSES, LAURENCE POUNTNEY HILL
1703

This is an example of the new type of housing that was built in the City after the Great Fire of 1666. The buildings are laid out in accordance with the medieval street plan, but they are made of brick and tiles rather than wood and straw. The houses, with a base clad in stone topped by three storeys of exposed brickwork, display restrained ornamentation, achieved through the use of relief and the interplay between stone and brick.

●3

●4 | WARDROBE PLACE
1710

This quiet corner of the City owes its name to its former use, as before the Great Fire it was the site of a mansion that contained the royal wardrobe. After the disaster, the configuration of courtyards characteristic of the medieval City was preserved to accommodate new housing created by master builders. Only numbers 3 and 5 date from 1710; the others were put up at a later date. The main elevation follows the model of the houses on Laurence Pountney Hill ●3, with a stone ground floor supporting three sparsely decorated storeys of brickwork.

●4

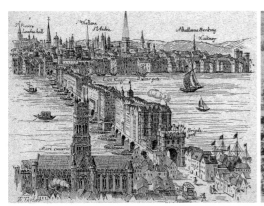
View of London Bridge
from the south bank

The Great Fire of London,
started on September 2

Map of the areas of the
city devastated by the Great Fire

1600   1666   1666

●5 | HOLBORN VIADUCT

1863 *William Heywood*

The unmanageable density of traffic endured by Fleet St. ●2 and the Strand in their role as the main links between Westminster and the City led to a decision to divert vehicles to the south, via the Embankment, and to the north, via the old Roman road that connected Marble Arch ▲04 with the General Post Office. The latter route involved the creation of New Oxford Street and the construction of this viaduct over the filled-in bed of the Fleet. Engineering goes hand in hand with architecture on this bridge, with its robust, beautifully ornamented iron girders and its buttresses, decorated in an Italianate style, which contain the steps leading to the viaduct. The outer pillars are crowned by four statues representing commerce, agriculture, science and the arts.

●5

●6 | SMITHFIELD MARKET

1866 *Horace Jones*

This Victorian building, on the site of an old cattle and horse market that started operating in the 12th century, now houses a thriving urban market specializing in meat and poultry. The sale of livestock was transferred to Islington in 1855, but Smithfield remained active in the new building designed by Jones. Its brick building clad in stone is embellished on its corners by octagonal towers ending in a dome. The market has four large sales areas, organized around three avenues with long lanterns. A fire in 1958 made it necessary to overhaul the building, while a more recent refurbishment has adapted the market to the prevailing requirements of the health and safety regulations.

●6

View of London
Canaletto

●7 | LEADENHALL MARKET

1879 *Horace Jones*

This market has been a meeting place for traders in poultry, fish and dairy products since the 14th century. In 1411 it was taken over by the City, which still runs it to this day. Its name refers to an old mansion house with a lead roof that was put up in the surrounding area in the 14th century. The market was partially destroyed in the Great Fire. In 1881 Horace Jones, who was responsible for other market buildings in London in his capacity as Architect for the Corporation of the City, designed the Victorian wrought-iron buildings with glass galleries that can still be seen today. Leadenhall stands on the former site of a great Roman basilica, considered at the time to be the most significant of its kind this side of the Alps.

●7

●8 | BARBICAN ESTATE

1959 *Chamberlin Powell and Bon*

This ambitious residential project was designed to offer professionals in the City housing close to their workplace, thereby repopulating the district. This area was practically devastated by the Blitz, although the construction work for the Barbican did also provide the opportunity to rebuild St. Giles' Church and brought to light part of the Roman wall. The complex's characteristic concrete towers house almost 4,000 people in 140 different types of home. Gardens and ponds articulate the residential complex, which has been complemented in recent years by the Barbican Centre, an underground cultural venue.

●8

44

Fragment of the Rhinebeck Panorama
English School

View of Ludgate Hill from Fleet Street
at the beginning of the 20th century

Present-day panoramic
view of the City at night

1806   **1900**   **2001**

●9

●9 | LONDON WALL

1963 *City of London Planning Department*
This office complex – made up of six tower blocks spread along two sides of a street – was planned in parallel with the construction of the Barbican. The buildings were put up on double-height podiums and linked by high bridges running across the street. This format was originally proposed for the reconstruction of the City but the idea was eventually discarded. Amidst the feverish speculation of the 1980s, the initial layout was modified by the refurbishment of several of the buildings and the construction of new ones, such as the colossal Lee House designed by Terry Farell.

●10

●10 | BROADGATE

1984 *Arup Associates; Skidmore, Owings and Merrill*
This office complex was built in two stages, the first stretching from 1984 to 1988, the second from 1988 to 1991. The Arup project drew inspiration from the approach of the 1950s and provided over 150,000 sq. m of office space that blended into the City landscape thanks to its moderate height and the public squares articulating the area. The second phase, instigated by SOM, followed the same pattern but introduced higher buildings, including the extension to the office consisting of new blocks like the 167-m-high (548-ft-high) Broadgate Tower.

View of the ensemble formed by the
Houses of Parliament and Westminster Abbey

N

Westminster

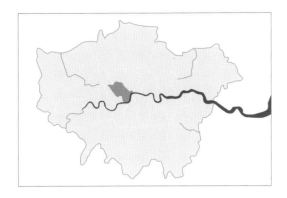

The United Kingdom's religious, administrative and legislative centre is bounded to the north and south by, respectively, the old Roman road of Oxford Street and the River Thames. Spread over 21 sq. km (8 sq. mi), Westminster boasts a population of 220,000 inhabitants. The district's capital importance was asserted as early as the 11th century by the presence of an abbey. Later on, the efforts of Henry VIII would endow it with some of the city's most important parks. The monumentality of the royal and government buildings is complemented by the orderly composition of the distinguished residences that have enlarged Westminster since the 17th century.

●11

●11 | ST. JAMES'S PARK
1550

Charles II turned one of Henry VIII's old hunting grounds into a park designed along French lines. The 57-acre park, bounded by the Mall ●15, the processional avenue leading to Buckingham Palace ■068, originally had an elegant rectangular canal, but in the 19th century John Nash set about drawing up St. James's Park in its current form, converting the canal into an irregularly shaped lake that has proved extremely popular with birds. The southern entrance is set off by a superb example of 18th-century domestic architecture, while the Royal Military Chapel and the Wellington Barracks, dating from the first three decades of the 19th century, stand further to the west.

●12

●12 | GREEN PARK
1550

To the north of Buckingham Palace ■068 lies this quiet park which, like St. James's Park ●11, once formed part of Henry VIII's hunting grounds. Spread over 40 acres, it connects Hyde Park ●13 with St. James's Park to create a large expanse of green in the heart of the city. The park was enclosed by Charles II in 1668 and in the following century it was converted into a garden, which was eventually opened to the public in 1826. All its buildings were removed in 1855, along with a pond, leaving today's unadorned esplanade of grass and trees.

●13

●13 | HYDE PARK
1550

The 350 acres of Hyde Park make it the biggest park in the city centre. Henry VIII bought it in 1536 as a hunting ground and Charles I opened it to the public in 1637. A century later, the flow of the River Westbourne was blocked to build the Serpentine, a lake spanning 27 acres. After the urbanisation of Belgravia and Pimlico, property developers set their sights on Kensington, Notting Hill and Bayswater, so the park ended up being surrounded by terrace houses with five or six storeys. Hyde Park has often served as a magnificent venue for large-scale concerts and festivals.

View of Westminster Abbey
and the surrounding area

Map of London, Westminster
and the surrounding area

●14 | COVENT GARDEN PIAZZA

1631 *Inigo Jones*

After the confiscation of the Church's assets in 1552, the garden formerly attached to St. Peter's Convent passed into the hands of the Earl of Bedford. In 1631 Jones came up with a classical design inspired by the Italian piazza. Its continuous façade conceals family homes set above arcades and dominated by St. Paul's Church ▲34. The piazza – the first of its kind to be built in London – quickly became a haunt of the gentry, but the opening of a market on the site in 1671 brought in a wider range of social classes. The Covent Garden Piazza was restored in the late 20th century and its old marketplace now contains a shopping mall.

●14

●15 | THE MALL

1660

This avenue formed part of the plan for St. James's Park ●11 and its surrounding roads instigated by Charles II and attributed to Louis XIV's landscape gardener, Le Nôtre. The Mall links Buckingham Palace ■068 with Trafalgar Square ● 21 and marks the boundary of St. James's Park. It is flanked by monumental buildings, including St. James's Palace ●55 and Marlborough House ■037. Carlton House Terrace ■069, built by John Nash, stands out on account of its coherent integration into the splendour of the avenue. Its current use as a processional route for the monarchy only arose in the 20th century, when the construction of the Admiralty Arch ■ 087 supplied a setting worthy of the royal family and guests.

●15

●16 | ST. JAMES'S SQUARE

1665

Henry Jermin was granted the ownership of this plot of land to reward his loyalty to Charles II during the latter's years of exile. Jermin developed it by creating a central square surrounded by various mansion houses, including his own residence. The result was an elegant, coherent ensemble featuring three-story buildings finished with brick, offset by details in stone. The sense of unity is enhanced by the restricted access, as open spaces are limited to the centres of the north, east and west sides. The buildings began to be reconstructed in the 18th century and the present-day façades are Georgian and neo-Georgian.

●16

Map of Westminster in the
early 20th century

Image of Nelson's Column,
in Trafalgar Square

1802   1850

● 17 | CAVENDISH SQUARE

1717 *John Price*

This was the first square to be built in the new residential neighbourhood of Marylebone. Its configuration determined the layout of the surrounding streets, as well as the symmetrical composition of Hanover Square on the other side of Oxford Street. Only two splendid buildings have survived from the 18th century to allow us to imagine Cavendish Square's original appearance, although it remains an elegant ensemble of noble proportions. Nearby, Vere Street contains the small St. Peter's Church, originally conceived as the square's parish church; although its architect, James Gibb, clearly drew on the work of Wren for the exterior, he was inspired by the recently built St. Martin's-in-the-Fields ■044 for the interior.

● 17

● 18 | GROSVENOR SQUARE

1720

Richard Grosvenor wanted to emulate the successful development of Hanover Square on his own property, which until then had been put to agricultural use. This ambitious project constituted, along with the streets that linked it with Hanover Square and Berkeley Square, the hub of Mayfair's urban configuration. Although the surrounding area still boasts some original houses with refurbished façades, Grosvenor Square itself has not preserved any of its initial buildings, which were rebuilt over the course of time to form, by the 20th century, a neo-Georgian ensemble comprising embassies, hotels and exclusive residences. The overall tone is offset, however, by the more modern appearance of the United States embassy, designed by Eero Saarinen.

● 18

Regent's Park and the
surrounding area

Image of the Crystal Palace,
standing in Hyde Park

The street market in the
Covent Garden Piazza

50

●19 | REGENT'S PARK

1812 *John Nash*

In 1809 Nash came up with an ambitious plan to transform the hunting ground of Marylebone Park into a forerunner of the garden city championed by the Arts and Crafts Movement: a park, surrounded by terrace houses, endowed with a lake, 56 villas and a second residence for the prince. Finally, a number of factors made it necessary to reduce the dimensions of Park Crescent ●20 and renounce most of the villas that had originally been foreseen. Since its opening in 1835, however, the 486-acre park has acquired new amenities, such as the zoo, the botanical garden and sports facilities.

●19

●20 | PARK CRESCENT

1812 *John Nash*

The main entrance to Regent's Park ●19 is marked by this row of terrace houses arranged in a crescent formation. Although the original plan anticipated the construction of a colossal circular structure, it was finally decided to opt for this semicircle in white stucco. The row of columns serves not only to support the continuous terrace on the first floor but also protects the individual entrances to the houses (now used as offices). The austerity of the block's ornamentation allows the focus of attention to fall on this colonnade.

●20

●21 | TRAFALGAR SQUARE

1820 *John Nash*

As part of the plan to renovate Charing Cross ▲26, Nash proposed creating a square on the confluence of Whitehall with the route that linked St. Paul's Cathedral ■028 and Buckingham Palace ■068. Nash designed only the eastern side of the square; the rest of the perimeter is outlined by what is now Canada House (drawn up by Smirke), on the west side; the National Gallery ▲41 (the work of Wilkins), to the north; two old Victorian hotels on the south side, now converted into offices, and St. Martin's-in-the-Fields ■044 to the east. In the centre, a large Corinthian column supports the statue of the hero of Trafalgar, Horatio Nelson, designed by William Railton and put up in 1842.

●21

View of Hyde Park Corner
in the late 19th century

Traffic on Westminster Bridge at the
start of the 20th century

Panoramic view of the central
area of Westminster

1890 **1926** **1930**

●22

●23

●24

●22 | BELGRAVE SQUARE

1825 *Thomas Cubitt*

The leafy trees occupying the central area in this square prevent it from being viewed as a whole but cannot disguise its impressive 19th-century elegance. The placement of the buildings sets Cubitt's project apart, as each of the four corners are marked by free-standing mansions adjacent to the roads leading to the square. The sides are lined with rows of four-story terrace houses. Cubitt's intention was to break away from the uniformity of the Georgian squares, as evidenced by the use of different motifs on each elevation and the individual design of all the entrances to the houses.

●23 | WILTON CRESCENT

1827 *Seth Smith*

This crescent of terrace houses constitutes the northern entrance to Belgravia, the prestigious residential neighbourhood drawn up by the property developer Thomas Cubitt in the 19th century. The view of the block from Hyde Park Corner was intended to alert visitors to the exclusive nature of the streets and squares around it. Unlike Nash's Park Crescent ●20, which opens on to Regent's Park ●19, this complex faces the buildings that surround one of the entrances to Belgrave Square ●22. The northern façade was clad in stone by Balfour and Turner at the beginning of the 20th century, while the south side has preserved the pilasters and stucco characteristic of Belgravia.

●24 | WATERLOO PLACE

1828 *John Nash*

Waterloo Place marks the start of Regent St., the triumphal way designed to connect the former residence of the Prince of Wales, Carlton House Terrace ■069, and the newly created Regent's Park ●19. The rear of the residential complex, markedly different from the main monumental façade, corresponds in terms of coherence and symmetry with the rest of Waterloo Place. The latter's intersection with Pall Mall is taken up by two clubs, the Athenaeum ■072, designed by Decimus Burton, and the United Services Club, originally designed by Nash and later refurbished by Burton.

Kensington Palace, with its gardens in the foreground
and farmlands in the background

The Thames with Chelsea College in the background
Canaletto

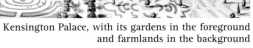

N

Kensington and Chelsea

Ladbroke Grove

Wood Lane

Westway

A 40 (M)

West Cross Route

Ladbroke Grove

32

28

Holland Park Av.

31 57
21

Uxbridge Road

10

Shepherd's Bush

Holland Rd.

High Street Kensington

86

85

Sloane St.

27

West Cromwell Road

Brompton Road

29

113

93

Hammersmith Road

Hammersmith Flyover

Old Brompton Road

43

44

26

101

33

25

33

118

30

Fulham Road

King's Road

62

79

34

Fulham Palace Road

Lillie Road

Dawes Road

Fulham Road

63

67

Hammersmith and Fulham

New King's Road

52

9

Kensington and Chelsea | Hammersmith and Fulham

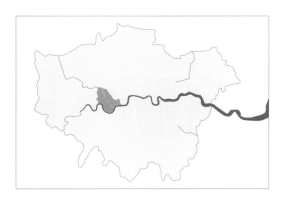

The borough of Kensington and Chelsea occupies a narrow strip spread over 12 sq. km (4½ sq. mi), bordering on Westminster to the east and Hammersmith to the west. The borough has a total of 174,000 residents. Chelsea, to the south, has traditionally been a refuge for intellectuals and artists, while Kensington, the site of the royal palace of the same name, has close links with the monarchy. The 16 sq. km (6⅕ sq. mi) of the neighbouring borough, Hammersmith and Fulham, maintained their agricultural character until the 19th century, when the expansion of London led to a construction boom the results of which now provide housing for 174,000 inhabitants.

●25

●25 | ROYAL AVENUE
1692
Royal Avenue is one of the various open squares that give on to King's Road. It was intended to be the opening section of a triumphal way leading from Wren's Royal Hospital ■033, close to the Thames, to Kensington Palace ■021, further to the north. This ambitious project of William III came to a halt in King's Road, a few hundred yards from the hospital. Royal Avenue now consists of a rectangular central garden bordered on its longitudinal sides by rows of 19th-century terrace houses.

●26

●26 | SLOANE SQUARE
1780 *Henry Holland (attributed)*
This square is named after Hans Sloane, the wealthy doctor and scientist who resided in Chelsea and owned a private collection that served as the initial impulse for the British Museum ■067. Despite numerous reconstructions of the buildings around it, Sloane Square has maintained a certain coherence and elegance. The newer buildings lining the central garden space include the department store Peter Jones ■101, a superlative example of 1930s' architecture. The opposite side is taken up by the Royal Court Theatre, which celebrated fifty years of staging groundbreaking plays in 2006.

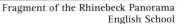

Fragment of the Rhinebeck Panorama
English School

Veterans read a report of the Battle of Waterloo
in front of the Royal Hospital, in Chelsea

●27 | EDWARDES SQUARE

1811

This square in the late Georgian style takes its name from William Edwardes, who rented this plot of land belonging to the Holland House estate. The exquisite delicacy of the small Tuscan temple in the central garden, spread over more than 2½ acres, contrasts with the austerity and small dimensions of the houses around the perimeter of the square. The north side is taken up by the back of the houses on Earls Terrace. The east and west sides are distinguished by terraces endowed with simple coherence, while the southern edge is lined with buildings in a range of styles.

●27

●28 | NORLAND SQUARE

1837 *Robert Cantwell*

Norland Square forms part of a meticulously planned composition remarkable for the balance and harmony of its various elements: crescents, avenues, squares and gardens. The terrace houses surrounding the central garden of Norland Square are characterized by its four-storey stucco façades decorated with cornices. The continuous galleries of the basement and ground floor support the balcony running along the first floor, which is protected by an iron balustrade. Queensdale and Princedale Streets connect this square with the nearby Royal Crescent, embellished by terrace houses similar to those in the square, the spacious Addison Avenue and the stone-clad buildings in St. James's Gardens.

●28

54

●29

●30

●29 | PELHAM PLACE, PELHAM CRESCENT
1840 *George Basevi*

Basevi, who was a disciple of Soane, was responsible for a good number of development projects scattered around Kensington. This residential composition is bounded by the triangle made up of Fulham Road, Pelham Street and Onslow Square. Pelham Place and Pelham Crescent share the same pattern of domestic architecture, with symmetrical three-storey houses complete with a basement and an attic set back from a balustrade, but the two projects also display specific distinguishing features. In Pelham Place, the houses are endowed with a front garden that recalls the residential neighbourhoods in the suburbs, while those of the Crescent, which is almost 150 m in diameter, are graced by small porches that protect their entrance.

●30 | BROMPTON CEMETERY
1840

In the 1820s, it became clear that measures were required to combat the city's unhealthy living conditions, exacerbated by the rapid increase in its population. The Brompton Cemetery was one of the first cemeteries to be built outside the central nucleus of London, as part of this process of sanitary reform. This resting ground, which occupies a flat, rectangular 40-acre plot, was consecrated in 1840. Its symmetrical composition – partly the work of Benjamin Baud – is particularly distinguished by its octagonal Anglican chapel with an imposing arched structure. A variety of styles can be discerned in the cemetery's 35,000-plus funeral monuments, with a predominance of neoclassical, Gothic and Egyptian designs.

Main façade of Kensington Palace
from Kensington Gardens

Kensington Gardens

●31 | KENSINGTON PALACE GARDENS

1843 *James Pennethorne*

In 1840 the agricultural land that provided sustenance for the royal family became available for building when the crops were transferred to Windsor. Property developers proposed the construction of a residential complex of elegant family mansions (each with an ample garden) that would run along both sides of an avenue over 20 m (65½ ft) wide. From 1840 to 1870 various architects helped make this prestigious project a reality, mainly with Italianate and Queen Anne-style designs. Wyatt and Brandon took charge of the entrances and numbers 18 and 19; Knowles drew up number 15; Decimus Burton, Sidney Smirke and James Murray were responsible for 12a, while Banks and Barry contributed numbers 12 and 18.

●31

●32 | LADBROKE ESTATE

1850 *Thomas Allom*

This housing estate is one of the most successful examples of Victorian city planning applied to the periphery of London. This complex of Italianate homes was immediately popular, thanks to its superb location on a hill and the unconventional, spacious layout of the buildings, which are organized around the central north-south axis of Ladbroke Grove, which goes up the hill and borders on Ladbroke Square. To the north of the latter lie Lansdowne Crescent, Elgin Crescent and Clarendon Road. The estate's buildings are distributed in groups of two or four houses, with back gardens leading to the parks reserved for the exclusive use of their occupants.

●32

Regatta on the Thames underneath
Albert Bridge

Dome of the Brompton Oratory,
in South Kensington

●33 | THE BOLTONS
1850

London's westward expansion in the mid-19th century manifested itself in the form of a series of residential complexes which, despite the predominant Italianate style, display specific features adapted to the setting and to possible eventual uses. The Boltons are distinguished by its enormous, semi-detached stuccoed villas, organized around a garden in the form of a mandala. In the centre of the complex stands St. Mary's, a church designed in 1850 with a floor plan in the form of a Greek cross.

●33

●34 | THAMES WHARF
1984 *Richard Rogers Partnership*

An old industrial complex that included a cluster of warehouses from the early 20th century served as the starting point for this multipurpose ensemble beside the Thames. An office block was set in a converted warehouse embellished by the addition of a spectacular vaulted roof spanning two storeys. This building also contains a restaurant with a panoramic view of the new public space that has been created on the river bank. The residential section comprises 25 homes, spread over three buildings that draw on the area's industrial past for inspiration. These blocks were designed in accordance with construction methods characteristic of the 1960s, and the distinctive final result is the sum of various elements with their own individual identity.

●34

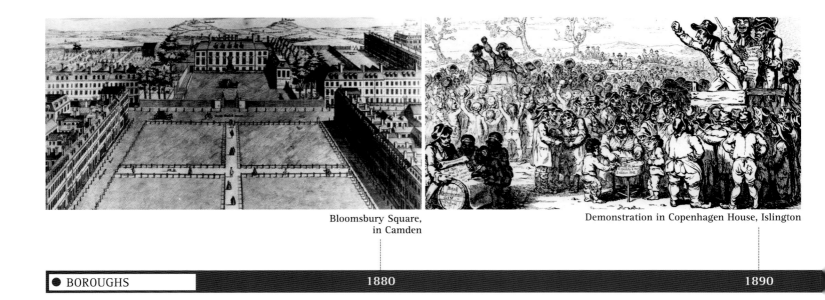

Bloomsbury Square,
in Camden

Demonstration in Copenhagen House, Islington

1880

1890

58

Islington

Hackney

Camden

The 22 sq. km (8½ sq. mi) of Camden offer a wide variety of geographical and architectural contrasts. Its population of 211,000 surpasses that of its neighbour, Islington, which accommodates 180,000 residents within its 15 sq. km (5⅘ sq. mi). The latter borough, to the north of the City, was, until the 19th century, wooded agricultural land that was popular with Londoners. Hackney, the most easterly of this trio, covers an area of 19 sq. km (7⅓ sq. mi), bounded to the east by the River Lea. Its 208,000 inhabitants are unevenly distributed over its territory.

●35

●35 | LINCOLN'S INN
1400

Lincoln's Inn is situated in the centre of the north-south axis linking the city's Inns of Court. It was founded in the 13th century as a Dominican monastery, before serving as a home to the Earl of Lincoln and finally, in the 14th century, becoming a residence for lawyers. Four open spaces connect a group of buildings from different periods that now house legal practices. The imposing main entrance, from 1518, is set in an original brick façade with recurring blue motifs. The east courtyard leads to the Old Buildings, a composition of brick volumes from the 16th and 17th centuries adjacent to the chapel, from the first third of the 17th century, and the old hall of the lawyers' residence, dating from 1492.

●36 | BLOOMSBURY SQUARE
1660

This was the first open square to be created in Bloomsbury as a result of the city's expansion towards the west. The square was originally named after the fourth Earl of Southampton, who rented out part of his lands to build the new residential neighbourhoods designed to house the city's growing population. Southampton House was put up to the north, while the rest of the perimeter was occupied by distinguished terrace houses. Years later, the Southampton inheritance passed by marriage into the hands of the Dukes of Bedford, who deserted Bloomsbury in the early 19th century when it fell out of favour with the gentry. The Bedford residence was demolished, along with the other original buildings, to make way for new terrace houses.

●36

The boroughs of Camden, Islington and Hackney

Fragment of the Rhinebeck Panorama
English School

●37 | HOXTON SQUARE
1683

Shoreditch was one of the first boroughs on the outskirts of London to merge with the city's historic centre. The continuous reconstruction in this area has made it impossible to preserve anything from the medieval or Tudor areas and the oldest buildings date from the 17th century. Hoxton Square is an example of the urban planning of that period, although none of its original buildings have survived to the present day. The square was opened up in an attempt by property developers to achieve an eastward expansion as successful and elegant as the one that was taking place on the opposite side of the city, but the progressive appearance of stores and workshops in the 19th century tarnished the district's prestige.

●37

●38 | NEW SQUARE
1690

New Square is situated between Carey Street, which borders the Royal Courts of Justice ■078, and Lincoln's Inn ●42. The abundance of members of the legal profession led the four-storey, U-shape building to be originally used as accommodation for lawyers, although the apartments were later converted into offices. A passage connects Carey Street with the garden area marked out by the U of the building, and this garden in its turn is linked to Lincoln's Inn. This layout is typical of the colleges of Oxford and Cambridge, which in fact may well have been the source of inspiration for the squares of London.

●38

Catholic school in
Lincoln's Inn Fields

London's expansion towards
the north of the City

1808

1845

●39

●39 | GEFFRYE MUSEUM
1715

The Ironmonger's Almshouses provided refuge for the needy until 1908. The buildings lining three sides of the large central courtyard originally contained 14 hospices, which were situated outside the city at the time of their foundation. On the side opposite the main entrance, the chapel, reached by an avenue flanked by lime trees, is the only building displaying elaborate ornamentation, as the rest of the ensemble is characterised by the austerity of the brickwork and the symmetry of the openings. The conversion of the almshouse into a museum by the LCC involved the elimination of the upper floor, as well as many of the staircases and party walls.

●40

●40 | CHURCH ROW
1720

Church Row, characterised by the spacious but anarchic layout of its architecture, is one of the best preserved Georgian streets in Hampstead. The terrace houses on the south side, which all date back to 1720, are embellished by large windows and subtle ornamentation, achieved merely with brickwork. In contrast, the buildings on the north side, bordering on Hampstead cemetery, vary in both their form and their date of construction. The leafy central strip that divides the street into two is an unusual feature in London urban design.

Autumn in Hampstead
John Atkinson Grimshaw

The British Museum after its
opening in Camden

●41 | BEDFORD SQUARE

1775 *Thomas Leverton (attributed)*

A century after the creation of Bloomsbury Square ●35, this space heralded a new era in the urbanisation of the Duke of Bedford's estate that would soon go on to embrace other squares, such as those of Russell ●39, Tavistock and Gordon. Bedford Square, which has survived virtually intact until the present, is surrounded by austere, four-storey terrace houses. The continuous brick façades, with their entrances adorned with stone, are interrupted in the centre of each side to make room for a residence clad with stucco and finished with a frontispiece supported by pillars. The buildings on the ends of the south sides are crowned with balustrades. These details endow the square with a distinguished appearance, making it look as if it is flanked by four palaces.

●41

●42 | RUSSELL SQUARE

1800 *James Burton, Humphrey Repton*

Russell Square, 210 m (689 ft) long and 205 m (673 ft) wide, is one of the biggest squares in London. The garden, designed by Repton, was originally surrounded by substantial terrace houses, some of which can still be seen, particularly on the south and east sides. The terracotta decorations were added well into the 19th century in an attempt to discourage the Victorian upper classes from deserting the Georgian Bloomsbury area in search of other more sophisticated neighbourhoods. The eastern façade has been occupied since 1898 by the opulent Hotel Russell, which stands opposite the colossal Art-Deco Senate House, now used as the offices of the University of London. The central garden, which was renovated in the 1960s with a new design, was reendowed with Repton's original composition in 2002.

●42

Street market in Islington

View of St. Giles' Circus, the meeting point
of the City and Camden

●43

●43 | BARNSBURY SQUARE
1820 *Thomas Cubitt*

Before going on to develop Belgravia and Bloomsbury,
Cubitt built this coherent residential composition of streets,
crescents and squares with open corners on both sides of
Thornhill Road. The complex still retains a good number of
its original buildings, as well as the spacious layout drawn
up by Cubitt. Mountford Crescent, to the north of
Barnsbury Square, boasts a pair of two-storey villas clad
with stucco and separated from the street by a private garden. Belitha Villas, to the north, and Richmond Avenue, to
the south, have preserved magnificent examples of terrace
houses from the period. Finally, to the west of Barnsbury
Square, the elliptical Thornhill Square is completed on the
northern side by Thornhill Crescent ●44.

●44

●44 | THORNHILL CRESCENT
1820 *Thomas Cubitt*

The urban development of the Thornhill estate began in
the early 19th century, but Thornhill Square was not built
until 1848. This square follows the format typical of
Cubitt, whose projects sought to break away from the
strict Georgian style by opening up squares on their sides.
In accordance with this scheme, Thornhill Crescent occupies only the northern side of the square, bordering the
top end of the ample central area. The three-floor terrace
houses combine stucco – on the ground floor and the decorations on the façade – and brick – on the other storeys.

●45

●45 | MILNER SQUARE
1841 *Roumieu and Gough*

The austere houses surrounding Milner Square add a continental touch to this square in Islington. The brick and
stucco elevations are characterised by a simple ground
floor supporting two storeys and an attic, which is set
apart by a continuous cornice. The three corridors running down each home are marked out by thin pillars that
combine with the narrow rectangular openings to emphasise the predominant verticality of the ensemble. The neo-
Gothic echoes in the square's architecture typify the style
adopted by Roumieu and Gough in the second half of the
19th century.

Panoramic view of the medieval city
and the first development towards the east

The Tower of London seen from the Thames

1650

1650

Tower Hamlets

N

Newham

Romford Rd.

High St. North

51
Bethnal Green

48

84
Whitechapel Rd.

Mile End Rd.

Manor Rd.

60

Barring Rd.

Newham Way

Commercial Rd.

East India Dock

50

9
2
64

120

122 54
127

129

Albert Rd.

53

43
58 Plumstead

55

Westferry Road

Evelyn St.

46
22 52

Greek Rd.
15
39 56

131
40 102

47

53

14

Hill Rd.

Rochester Way

Academy Rd.

Shooters Hill

45

36
49

Lewisham

Greenwich

Tower Hamlets | Newham | Greenwich | Lewisham

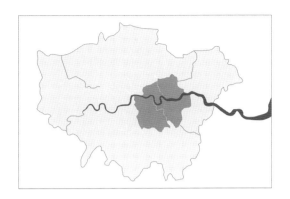

The docks of Tower Hamlets and Newham, to the east of the City, have experienced a dramatic transformation since their closure in the 1980s. The 20 sq. km (7¾ sq. mi) of Tower Hamlets accommodate 207,000 inhabitants, while Newham possesses a total of 36 sq. km (14 sq. mi) and 251,000 residents. Over the river, on the south bank, lie Lewisham and Greenwich. The former has 35 sq. km (13½ sq. mi) and 248,000 inhabitants, while the latter spans 47 sq. km (18 sq. mi) and is home to 224,000 people, as well as a rich architectural heritage.

●46

●46 | ROYAL NAVAL HOSPITAL

1664 *Christopher Wren, Nicholas Hawksmoor, John Vanbrugh, John Webb*

Webb came up with a composition of three buildings arranged around a courtyard opening on to the river for the refurbishment of an old Tudor palace in Greenwich. Only the west wing was completed, but this served as Wren's starting point in 1695 for the construction of a residence for retired naval officers. He put up a building identical to Webb's on the opposite side of the central space and set two further blocks behind it, facing each other in the form of a 'U' and closed off by a splendid colonnade. Hawksmoor and Vanbrugh, two of Wren's pupils, continued his project, which took several decades to bring to fruition. The interior is distinguished by the main hall, where Hawksmoor's baroque design matches to perfection the wall paintings by Sir James Thornhill.

●47

●47 | GREENWICH PARK

1690 *Inigo Jones (attributed)*

Greenwich Park, spread over 183 acres, is set on high ground that has been occupied since Roman times. Its strategic location provides a panoramic view of both the City and the Thames. The estate passed into the hands of the royal family in the 15th century and has been witness to the lives of numerous monarchs. James I gave the land to his wife, Queen Anne, who in 1616 commissioned Inigo Jones to build the Palladian Queen's House, later enlarged by Charles II in 1664. The park, which has been declared a world heritage site, also contains Wren's Royal Observatory, perched on the top of the hill. The French-style design of the gardens is attributed to André le Nôtre, who was also responsible for Versailles.

Eastward expansion of the city
after the Great Fire

View of the Royal Hospital in Greenwich
from the Thames

●48 | ALMSHOUSES

1695

The Trinity House organisation, which is still active today, created this refuge for retired sailors and naval widows at the end of the 17th century. The complex, a magnificent example of the era's urban design, consists of two rows of single-storey brick houses arranged on either side of a leafy central avenue leading to the old chapel. This was decorated with an 18th-century ornamental panel from Bradmore House in Hammersmith. The bombardments of World War II razed the complex to the ground, but the land was purchased in 1954 by the London County Council (LCC) to turn into housing.

●48

●49 | THE PARAGON

1790 *Michael Searles*

The enormous Paragon complex comprises seven pairs of semi-detached houses in the form of a crescent, linked by a single-storey Tuscan colonnade. The ends of this colonnade are marked by lodge houses designed in the same style as the residences. The ensemble embodies the culmination of the Georgian style, with stone ornamentations on the façade, arched windows on the ground floor and attics jutting over the parapet. The rear façade is distinguished by its superb glass galleries. The nearby Paragon House is a more opulent, free-standing version of the houses on the crescent. The complex was rebuilt after the bombardments of World War II and converted into flats.

●49

The boroughs of Tower Hamlets, Newham, Greenwich and
Lewisham at the start of the 19th century

View of the Thames
from Greenwich

●50

●50 | ALBERT GARDENS
1810

In the late 18th and early 19th centuries, the need arose for a road connecting the City with the docks. Commercial Road, which corresponds to the section passing through Tower Hamlets, was opened between 1803 and 1810, and the same period saw the beginnings of urban development around the thoroughfare. Albert Gardens, which formed part of this expansion, is made up of a perfectly conserved square with a garden, bounded by a series of three-storey terrace houses and arched openings on the ground floor. The houses were refurbished by Anthony Richardson and Partners in the 1970s.

●51

●51 | BOUNDARY STREET ESTATE
1897 *LCC Architects Department*

This estate was one of the first urban renewal projects initiated by the LCC, which shared the zeal of Victorian philanthropists to do away with the slums. The area centred on Nichols Street had a particularly bad reputation, as reflected in Arthur Morrison's novel *A Child of the Jago*. The LCC came up with a radial system organised around Arnold Circus, a central square from which all the other streets ran off. The 23 five-storey blocks, inspired by the architecture of the Arts and Crafts Movement, could accommodate over 5,000 people. Red brick is the dominant element on the façades, which culminate in double-slope roofs. The complex also included communal facilities such as shops and schools.

Greenwich seen from across the Thames, with the hospital and observatory in the background

View of the Tower of London from the south

●52 | HOUSES, TRAFALGAR ROAD

1965 *James Gowan*

The Scots architect Gowan designed this low residential complex in the final stages of his partnership with James Stirling. Gowan borrowed elements from Victorian tradition and combined them with features typical of the modern architecture of the 1930s. The redbrick façades and simple metal-framed windows echo the latter period, while the use of street-level passageways to reach the houses reflects a desire to draw on the skills of the previous century. The simple geometric forms of the elevations contain the galleries and bridges that interconnect the buildings, which are organised around a central courtyard.

●52

●53 | THAMES BARRIER

1984 *GLC Department of Architecture*

Over the course of its history London has suffered from flooding on several occasions as a result of sudden increases in the level of the Thames. This phenomenon, caused by specific meteorological conditions, provoked an urgent need for a series of barriers on the river to check any possible onrush of water. The Thames Barrier, 520 m (1706 ft) in length, is the biggest of these protective structures. Nine concrete pillars stretching from bank to bank divide the river into ten channels, each guarded by movable steel gates that are left open when not in use, in order to allow vessels to pass through. The distinctive curved steel structures concealing the machinery on each pillar have transformed the appearance of the river on its way through Woolwich.

●53

The docks in the
mid-20th century

The King George V and Royal Albert Docks
when still in operation

Panoramic view of the Docklands
at the close of the 20th century

1950　　　　　　　　　**1960**　　　　　　　　　**1994**

●54

●54 | CANARY WHARF

1988 Skidmore Owings and Merrill

The construction of the Canary Wharf complex on the old docks endowed the city with a new neighbourhood devoted to business and leisure. The space, organized around a well-planned network of roads, is divided into 26 lots, mainly set around the perimeter of the dock and above the water. The highest buildings occupy the central core, while the low and medium-height volumes are situated closer to the river. The perimeter is devoted to office space, which surrounds the linear composition of a hub designed for leisure activities, green spaces and public amenities. The extension of the Docklands Light Railway and the Jubilee Line has boosted the development of the area in the last twenty years, to such an extent that it now plays host to over 55,000 workers.

●55

●55 | ISLE OF DOGS NEIGHBOURHOOD

1991 Chassay Architects

The crisis in the property market in the mid-1980s was followed by increased public investment aimed at completing the regeneration process in the old port area. The London Docklands Development Corporation (LDDC) held a competition to provide new amenities for Tower Hamlets, one of the few projects in this area financed by public money. This complex, easily identified by the rotunda in front of it, contains the head offices of various local bodies, including the striking cylindrical building that houses the offices of Tower Hamlets Council.

View of Southwark and London Bridge
in the Middle Ages

Springtime in Vauxhall Gardens

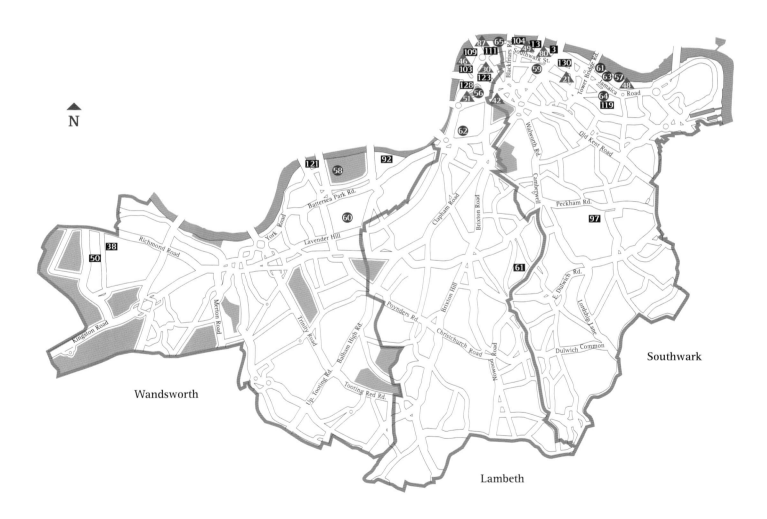

N

Southwark

Wandsworth

Lambeth

Southwark | Lambeth | Wandsworth

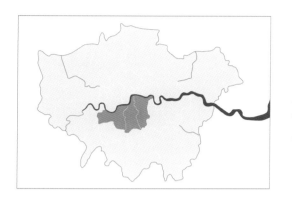

These three boroughs are situated on the south bank of the Thames, facing the section of the river stretching from Hammersmith to Tower Hamlets. The 34-sq.-km (13-sq.-mi) borough of Wandsworth, the most westerly of the trio, contains various hubs of population, with a total of 274,000 residents. Lambeth, in the middle, is a trapezoidal area spanning 27 sq. km (10½ sq. mi), growing wider as it moves away from the river. Its population is 269,000. Finally, Southwark, to the east, is a triangular borough measuring 29 sq. km (11 sq. mi), with 254,000 inhabitants and a long architectural history, as it was the site of the first settlements on the south bank.

●56

●56 | ARCHBISHOP'S PARK
1297

The 10 acres of Archbishop's Park were officially opened to the public in 1901, although the area's most impoverished children had been allowed to enter in the previous century. The park is situated to the east of Lambeth Palace ▲51, the residence of the Archbishops of Canterbury. The palace gardens, designed by John Nash, are the setting for this group of buildings in the medieval, Tudor and Jacobean styles, which is reached by an imposing redbrick entrance. The Archbishop's quarters were renovated in a neo-Tudor style in 1829, but the rest of the complex has maintained its original appearance. Particularly worthy of note are the 17th-century hall, which combines classical and Gothic elements, and the chapel, dating from 1228.

●57

●57 | BUTLER'S WHARF
1850 *Conran Roche*

To the east of Tower Bridge lies Shad Thames, an'alleyway running parallel to the river that was once the hub of the city's most important group of warehouses. When these were closed in the 1970s, the street, distinguished by the high bridges that served to deliver goods from one warehouse to another, fell into a decline that was only reversed by its conversion into a residential and leisure area. Terence Conran's project for this area spanning over 10 acres, organised around a central square and a riverside promenade, included the Design Museum ▲48, set in an old 1950s' warehouse, and the Butler's Wharf Building, an imposing refurbished building that now contains 88 flats.

Fire in the Albion Mill, at the southern end of Blackfriars Bridge

Panoramic view of Battersea and Chelsea, with central London in the distance

●58 | BATTERSEA PARK

1853 *James Pennethorne, John Gibson*

After completing Victoria Park in Hackney, Pennethorne turned to this new public space spread over nearly 200 acres, working in collaboration with Gibson, who was responsible for the design of the gardens. The marshy river bank was filled in with soil taken from other construction projects to create an embankment – one of the great feats of Victorian engineering. The park features elements typical of the period, such as the irregularly shaped lake, the main avenue and the floral compositions, as well as fountains built for the Festival of Britain in 1951. In the face of the government's reluctance to provide funding, the project was partially financed by the sale of terrace houses overlooking the park on Albert Bridge Road and Prince of Wales Drive.

●58

●59 | CENTRAL BUILDINGS

1866 *R. H. Moore*

This building designed to trade hops and malt, officially opened in 1868, was put up in the heart of London's breweries. The only survivor of the Victorian exchanges that played such an important role in 19th-century commerce consisted of a huge auction room with a glass roof. This central space was surrounded all the way round by continuous galleries supported by an impressive iron structure decorated with hop-plant motifs. In 1918 a fire destroyed the roof and part of the upper floors, but a painstaking reconstruction allowed the exchange – now used for offices – to recover its original design.

●59

The boroughs of Southwark, Lambeth and Wandsworth
at the start of the 19th century

Fragment of the Rhinebeck Panorama of London
English School

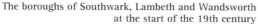

1802   1806

● 60

● 60 | SHAFTESBURY PARK ESTATE
1872

A co-operative called the Artisans, Labourers and General
Dwelling Company put up this large residential complex
with the aim of providing decent housing for the working
class. It boasts over 1,000 rented houses, arranged alongside leafy streets covering an area of 40 acres in all. The
two-storey buildings vary with respect to the number of
bedrooms and the design of their façades, but the overall
tone is set by neo-Gothic elements like the turrets on the
end houses and the paired entrances protected by a double-slope portico. Although the initial plan also anticipated the construction of a park and various communal
facilities, financial difficulties ultimately led to the rejection of some of the planned features.

73

● 61

● 61 | COURAGE'S BREWERY
1891

This old brewery formed part of a series of warehouses on
Shad Thames that were rebuilt after being destroyed by a
fire in 1891. A century later, the entire area was subjected
to a comprehensive urban development that showed off
the area's Victorian architecture by putting it alongside
contemporary projects. After closing the brewery in 1981,
Courage sold the building for conversion into housing.
The process of laying the foundations unearthed a wide
range of archaeological remains, including vestiges of the
first Globe Theatre, which was reconstructed and opened
to the public in 1996. The old brewery, which has conserved original elements like the white tower crowned by
a cupola, now houses the Tower Bridge Piazza complex.

Fisherman on the Thames
near Battersea Bridge

Lambeth, and its bank on the Thames,
seen from Millbank Street

74

●62 | COURTENAY SQUARE

1914 *Adshead and Ramsay*

Courtenay Square forms part of a larger residential complex on the grounds of the Cornwall Estate that was intended to replace the slums in this area on the south bank. The project also embraced part of Courtenay Street, Cardigan Street and Newburn Street. The two-storey terrace houses were based on the Regency model, with entrance porches protected by wooden lattices. The conversion of slums into modest homes inspired by the dominant style of the previous century contrasted with other initiatives of the time that explored recent architectural trends.

●62

●63 | HORSELYDOWN SQUARE

1986 *Wickham and Associates*

Southwark's meticulously reconstructed architectural gems from various eras rub shoulders with examples of cutting-edge modern architecture, such as this multipurpose complex in a pedestrian area next to Tower Bridge. Apart from four housing blocks, the Wickham project also includes two office buildings, shops on the ground floor and an underground car park. The distinctive forms of the façades, five to seven storeys high, reflects the innovative designs of late-20th-century Dutch cities and sets off the painstakingly faithful restorations of the old brick warehouses dotted along the south bank.

●63

Panoramic view of the growth of the
neighbourhoods in the south of the city

The South Bank
in the mid-19th century

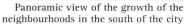

1845   1955

● 64

● 64 | THE CIRCLE

1987 *CZWG Architects, R. Keefe and Devane*
This multipurpose complex combines forthright modernity
with traditional elements of London architecture. It consists of 302 flats, shopping premises, a restaurant and a
gymnasium. The conventional layout of the ground floor
– a circular entrance courtyard – contrasts with the
groundbreaking design of the elevations. The façade of
the patio, clad with electric-blue bricks, culminates in a
striking parapet in the form of an owl, while the elevations on the street, although covered with typical brickwork, sport a wavy parapet. The diagonal mullions of the
windows and the structure supporting the balconies add
further distinctive touches to the building.

75

● 65 | SOUTH BANK

The southern bank of the Thames has experienced a great
transformation in recent decades between Waterloo ▲ 68
and London Bridge. Once an overwhelmingly industrial
area barely visited by most of the capital's inhabitants,
the South Bank has opened up to the river, offering a
large number of cultural and leisure facilities in the
process. Going eastward from Waterloo, the first attraction is the Jubilee Park, under the shadow of a colossal
Ferris wheel, the London Eye ■ 129. The embankment
then runs on to the powerhouse of London's performing
arts, the South Bank Centre and the Royal National
Theatre ▲ 87, which stand adjacent to the multipurpose
Gabriel's Wharf complex and the Oxo Tower shopping
centre. Blackfriars Bridge ▲ 62 marks the frontier between
the South Bank and Bankside, which has similarly been
turned into an area devoted to leisure and culture.

● 65

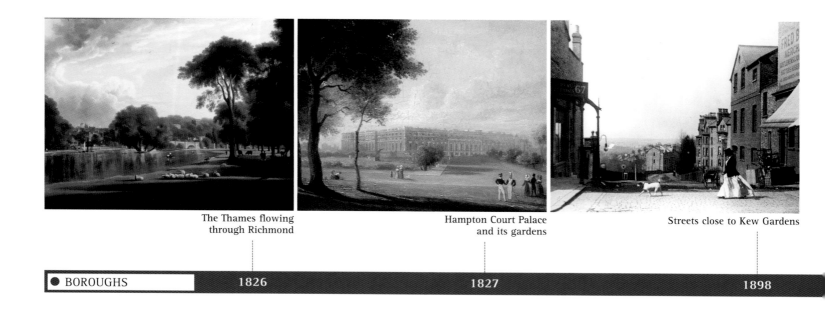

The Thames flowing
through Richmond

Hampton Court Palace
and its gardens

Streets close to Kew Gardens

● BOROUGHS   1826   1827   1898

N

Harrow

Brent

Hillingdon

Ealing

68

67

66
76

Richmond upon Thames

Hounslow

54

Outer West London

Brent, Ealing, Harrow, Hillingdon, Hounslow, Richmond upon Thames

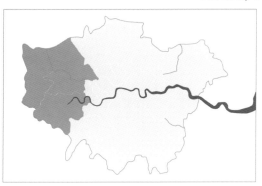

Until the mid-19th century the Outer West of London, which embraces a total of 378 sq. km (146 sq. mi) and 1,424,000 inhabitants, was a rural area dotted with mansion houses, like those of Chiswick ■045, Syon and Kew, and the villages that grew up around them. The Victorian era saw the emergence of the first residential neighbourhoods, which went on to expand over the course of the 20th century with the arrival of the underground railway. The outstanding architectural features are public and industrial buildings from the 1930s, as well as Wembley Stadium and Heathrow Airport (undoubtedly the main impetus for the area's development).

●66 | ROYAL BOTANIC GARDENS, KEW

This splendid 300-acre park is situated on the south bank of the Thames. Its origins can be traced back to a few early specimens that were planted around Kew Palace in 1696. George II founded a small 7½-acre botanical garden in 1759, then George III oversaw the merger of the estates of Kew and Richmond, which gave rise to William Chambers' designs for a series of exotic constructions. In 1841 the garden passed into the hands of the State, and in the following decades it was augmented by a pond and the Palm ■076 and Temperate Houses. Kew is now famous not only for its herbarium and its vast collection of live plants but also for its research centre.

●66

●67 | STOCKLEY PARK

1985 *Arup, SOM, Foster and Partners, Troughton McAslan, Geoffrey Darke, Ian Ritchie, Peter Foggo, Eric Parry, Charles Funke*

An old rubbish dump served as the basis for this office complex, which now plays host to over 30 companies. The area had to be prepared by removing over 18 million cubic metres of waste material – a titanic feat undertaken by Arup Associates. The subsequent landscaping determined the distribution and appearance of the buildings in the park. Of a total of 370 acres, 100 are given over to parkland and playing fields, while the remainder is taken up by offices and amenities.

●67

●68 | RICHMOND RIVERSIDE

1988 *Erith and Terry*

This urban complex was a response to the need to conserve two buildings in Richmond's historic centre. Breaking with the City's model of glass and concrete, Richmond Riverside provided a bright, modern, medium-size office space hidden behind façades that blend into the Georgian and Victorian setting. The complex is made up of a series of newly built terrace houses set around the pedestrian area of Heron Square. The elevations, inspired by the eclecticism of the Picturesque movement, start from a common Georgian base embellished by individual details in a baroque, neoclassical or Gothic style.

●68

View of Hampstead Heath
with London in the background

Highgate Road, which provides access
to London from the north

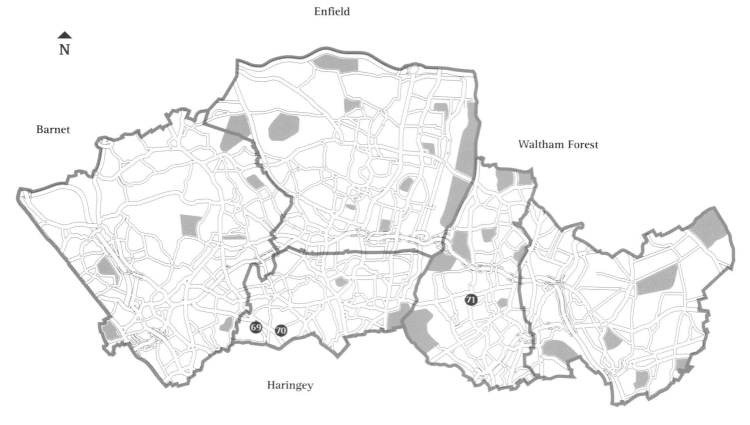

Enfield

N

Barnet

Waltham Forest

Haringey

Redbridge

Outer North London
Barnet, Enfield, Haringey, Redbridge, Waltham Forest

With the exception of various mansion houses and the occasional village founded between the 17th and 18th centuries, the urbanisation of these five boroughs mainly occurred in the 20th century. The development of the Underground in the first third of the century prompted the appearance of new residential neighbourhoods that were distinguished by several buildings with a modern design. To the east of this group of boroughs, which cover a total of 293 sq. km (113 sq. mi) with a population of 1,579,715, lies the large natural park of the Lea Valley.

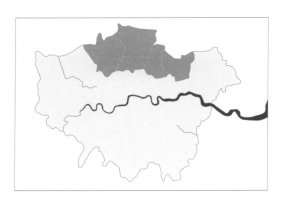

●69

●69 | HIGHGATE
1750

Although Highgate was already graced by the presence of mansions belonging to rich Londoners in the 16th century, it remained detached from the capital until the late 19th century, although the two previous centuries had seen the emergence of several clusters of population that would eventually shape the present-day neighbourhood. The Grove and Pond Square were among the first complexes to appear on Highgate Hill. The terrace houses on the Grove, dating from the 17th century, were arranged around a small park, while Pond Square, was made up of tiny terrace houses. The nearby South Grove boasts more ostentatious residences, while several 18th-century houses can still be seen on the High Street.

●70 | ARCHWAY
1900 *Alexander Binnie*

This viaduct was set above Archway Road, which was built in the 19th century to go round Highgate Hill. The original brick bridge was designed by John Nash in 1813, but at the turn of the century it was replaced by a new viaduct situated slightly further south. The great height of the bridge, with its superb wrought-iron ornamentation at each end, offers a stunning panoramic view of modern London.

●70

●71 | WALTHAMSTOW CIVIC CENTRE
1937 *P. D. Hepworth*

In 1932 the RIBA held a competition to design this centre. Hepworth came up with a group of three buildings complemented by two sports grounds, but the restrictions caused by the outbreak of World War Two made it necessary to reduce the scope of the initial plans. Although the construction date may suggest a neo-Georgian or even modern style, the two main buildings, which are clad in Portland stone, in fact embody a late version of the official Scandinavian architecture of the 1920s. The council building is adorned with a slender portico and three rows of openings, while the assembly hall, situated to the right of the central square, sports a more robust portico decorated with a frieze.

●71

James II being robbed on the banks of the Thames

Red House, the William Morris villa to the east of London

Car race heading towards Kent

1688

1980

1924

N

Havering

Barking and Dagenham

73

72

74

Bexley

Outer East London
Barking and Dagenham, Bexley, Havering

These three boroughs form part of the Thames Gateway, a reconstruction plan involving old industrial and dockland areas to the east of London. Barking and Dagenham, with 36 sq. km (14 sq. mi) and 166,000 inhabitants, and Havering, with 112 sq. km (43 sq. mi) and 225,000 inhabitants, have been part of Essex since 1965. Similarly, Bexley, with an area of 61 sq. km (24 sq. mi) and 219,000 residents, was once part of the primarily agricultural county of Kent, and even today it is characterised by a mixture of rural and urban settings.

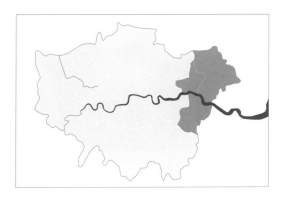

●72

●72 | LESNES ABBEY RUINS, THAMESMEAD
1178

After this monastery was founded in the 12th century, the boggy terrain on which it was built proved to be a source of problems. By the 14th century the institution could not meet the high maintenance costs occasioned by its riverside location and the site began to deteriorate. After the royal edict of 1524 that followed Henry VIII's breach with Rome, the monastery was dissolved and the new owners demolished most of its buildings. In 1930 the London County Council purchased the remains of the abbey, which went on to form part of the park that bears its name. The ruins reveal a composition distinct from other abbeys of the period, possibly as a result of its inconvenient location.

●73

●73 | WINDMILL, ST. MARY'S LANE
1790

This windmill, which was in operation until 1934, stands in the relatively new settlement of Upminster, which preserved its rural character until the 20th century. The picturesque windmill has been meticulously restored and has served as an important tourist attraction since the 1960s. It constitutes the area's scanty historical heritage, along with its most illustrious neighbour, the church.

●74

●74 | BECONTREE HOUSING ESTATE
1921

This residential complex was the most substantial public housing programme undertaken by the London County Council, which purchased 2,965 acres of agricultural land spread over Barking, Dagenham and Ilford for this purpose. Between 1921 and 1935, it built 25,000 new homes here to provide accommodation for 100,000 people. Both the urban development of the terrain and the buildings' façades were inspired by Welwyn Garden City and Hampstead Garden Suburb, although the architectural results were not as satisfactory. Even so, the houses boasted a gas, electricity, a bathroom and private gardens – all luxuries for the impoverished citizens of the interwar period.

Croydon Catholic Church

Donkey race in Wimbledon

N

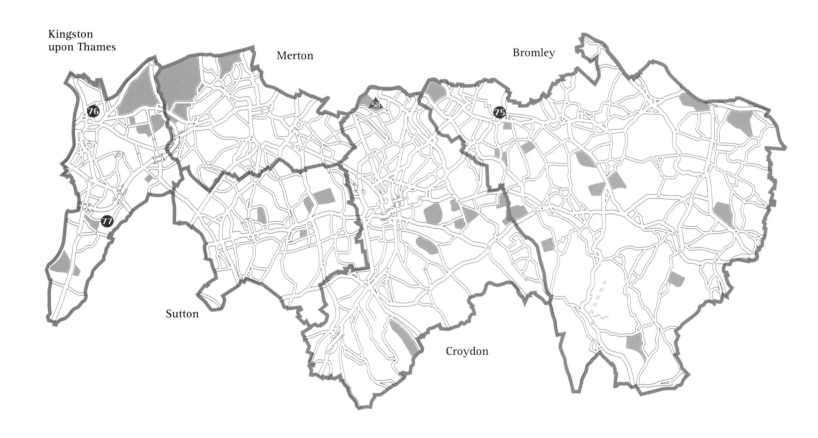

Kingston
upon Thames

Merton

Bromley

Sutton

Croydon

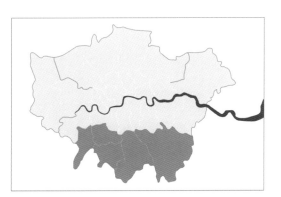

Outer South London
Bromley, Croydon, Kingston upon Thames, Merton, Sutton

The Outer South of London embraces five boroughs that occupy a total of 355 sq. km (137 sq. mi) and claim 1,155,000 inhabitants. It once comprised scattered villages and residential neighbourhoods founded in the early 18th century, but much of the area was absorbed by the urban expansion of the 19th century and the subsequent construction of new railway lines and roads. Nevertheless, these districts' proximity to the agricultural counties to the south (to which they once belonged) gives them a rustic touch that contrasts with the newer urban hubs.

● 75

● 75 | BROMLEY COLLEGE
1666

This institution was founded by the Bishop of Rochester as a refuge for vicars' widows. The complex now houses retired clergymen and their wives. The entrance to the premises is flanked by two pillars and crowned by an ornate frontispiece. The twenty original buildings, which have been converted into flats, are arranged around a square courtyard with an arched gallery running around the perimeter. The original chapel, restored in 1863 by Waring and Blake, features impressive stained-glass windows depicting female characters from the Old and New Testaments.

● 76

● 76 | MARKET PLACE
1838

Kingston market became an important trading centre as a result of a royal decree forbidding the opening of any other market within a radius of six miles. In the middle stands Market House, which served as the offices of Kingston's council from 1838 to 1935. All its four façades are adorned with two frontispieces and the weightiness of its mass is reduced by the addition of four square towers. The balustrade is topped by a statue of Queen Anne, sculpted by Francis Bird in 1706. Although the Market House is now used as a tourist office, the lively street market still takes place around it every day.

● 77

● 77 | HOGSMILL RIVER

This tributary of the Thames runs into the Thames in Kingston, which in 2002 set into motion a programme to regenerate the river valley by turning it into a leisure area. The idea was to turn the edges of the Hogsmill into a pedestrian walkway linking the town of Kingston to the southern part of the borough. At the confluence of the Hogsmill and the Thames, the banks of both rivers have been renovated to create a recreational area beside the water. The urban stretch of the Hogsmill has been transformed in order to highlight its importance in the context of Kingston, and the upriver barriers that blocked its course down the valley have been removed.

Monuments

Although archaeological excavations have unearthed traces of Roman monuments, the Saxons and Normans were not particularly fond of this type of construction. The main trigger for the emergence of monumental art in the city proved to be the opening of the first public urban parks in the course of the 16th and 17th centuries. The classicism of that period – with its exaltation of the individual and its inspiration in the sculptural powerhouses of Greece and Rome – encouraged the development of monumental ensembles. Later on, the monumentalist architecture of the Georgian and Victorian eras, along with the rise of neoclassicism, prompted the appearance of triumphal arches, columns and memorials to the dead. The colonial victories in the 19th century and the bloody world wars in the first half of the 20th century gave rise to the construction of numerous monuments in honour of war heroes.

86

▲01 | MONUMENT
City
1671 *Christopher Wren, Robert Hooke*
The 62-m (203-ft) height of this Doric column, erected to commemorate the Great Fire of 1666, is the equivalent of the distance that separates it from the old bakery where the disaster was sparked off. The Portland-stone pillar arises from a pedestal decorated with the handles of the city's taps, while the copper urn on the top symbolises the raging fire.

▲02 | SCREEN
Westminster
1825 *Decimus Burton*
The construction boom that followed the Battle of Waterloo in 1815 led to the embellishment of Hyde Park Corner, considered to be the western entrance to London. The subtle, elegant Screen that faces Constitution Arch (also designed by Burton) consists in its turn of three arches linked by a series of Ionic columns. The central arch is topped by a sculptural frieze designed by John Henning Junior.

▲03 | CONSTITUTION ARCH
Westminster
1827 *Decimus Burton*
The Corinthian solidity of this former gateway to Buckingham Palace ■068, crowned by an imposing depiction of Victory riding a bronze chariot, contrasts with the horizontal emphasis of the Screen. Before being transferred to its current location in 1883, the arch formed part of an orthogonal composition next to the southern entrance to Hyde Park ●13, along with other structures dating from the first third of the 19th century.

▲04 | MARBLE ARCH
Westminster
1828 *John Nash*
This monument, based on the Roman model of three arches and an elaborate sculptural ornamentation, was originally set in front of Buckingham Palace ■068, before being moved to the east of Hyde Park ●13 in 1851. Its white marble, which contrasted with the Bath stone of the royal residence, proved an ideal material for rendering the detail on the reliefs decorating the arches.

▲05 | DUKE OF YORK'S COLUMN
Westminster
1831 *Benjamin Wyatt*
This Tuscan column presides over the monumental ensemble of Waterloo Place ●24 and marks the southern end of the triumphal way planned to run from Nash's Carlton House Terrace ■069 to Regent's Park ●19. A large flight of steps rises up to the base of the robust pillar, which is crowned by a cupola supporting a statue of the Duke of York.

▲01   ▲05

▲03

▲04

▲06

▲08

▲09

▲06 | ALBERT MEMORIAL
Westminster
1863 *George Gilbert Scott*
This commemorative monument, situated at the entrance to Kensington Gardens, honours the memory of Queen Victoria's consort, who died in 1861. The ensemble, designed in Gothic style, features not only a huge statue of Prince Albert but also several friezes and groups of sculptures symbolising the scientific and cultural achievements of the prosperous Victorian era.

▲07 | QUEEN VICTORIA MEMORIAL
Westminster
1901 *Aston Webb, Thomas Brock*
Webb designed a setting to show off the commemorative monument to Queen Victoria produced by Brock. Situated between Buckingham Palace ■068 and the Mall ●15, the sculptural ensemble rises up from granite steps guarded by various bronze figures. The marble base supports several sculptures, including those of the Queen, which surround the tower crowned by a golden statue representing Victory.

▲08 | THE CENOTAPH
Westminster
1919 *Edwin Lutyens*
Lutyens, the epitome of the imperial architect, was chosen to design this cenotaph in tribute to the dead of the World War I. In 1919 a provisional monument was made with wood and plaster to commemorate the first anniversary of the armistice, and the following year the definitive version was built in Portland stone, with classical lines and meticulous attention to detail.

▲09 | MERCANTILE MARINE MEMORIAL
Tower Hamlets
1922 *Edwin Lutyens, Edward Maufe*
This memorial was built in two stages: one for sailors killed in the World War I, and another for those who died in World War II. The former, the work of Lutyens, consists of a temple crowned with a barrel vault and closed by a colonnade. For the latter, Maufe designed an ensemble comprising a flight of steps leading down to a garden.

▲10 | THAMES WATER RING MAIN TOWER
Hammersmith
1994 *Damien O'Sullivan, Tania Doufa*
The city's water system includes various safety pipes that stand 15 m (49 ft) above street level. In order to integrate one such tower into the bustling urban context of Shepherd's Bush, two students from the Royal College of Art proposed covering it with an enormous glass barometer. The level of the blue liquid inside serves to forecast the weather.

▲07

▲10

87

▲06 | Albert Memorial
George Gilbert Scott

The magnificence of this commemorative monument reflected the general sense of loss after the sudden death of Prince Albert. The main structure, a square, 53 m high (174 ft) Gothic tower decorated with angels, culminates in a slender pinnacle adorned with incrustations of precious stones. The pedestal that supports both the statue of Albert and the tower around it is raised in its turn on a platform that can be reached via four flights of granite steps. The ensemble is bordered by eight groups of sculptures. Four of these, made in bronze and set on the corners of the pedestal, represent the imperial colonies spread over America, Asia, Europe and Africa. The four on the platform, made of marble, embody the Victorian triumphs in the fields of commerce, agriculture, manufacturing and engineering. The frieze that runs round the perimeter of the pedestal depicts outstanding figures from all the arts, dating back to the time of Ancient Egypt, and is remarkable for its high degree of detail.

DISTRICT Westminster
LOCATION Kensington Gardens
DATE OF CONSTRUCTION 1863

Perspective

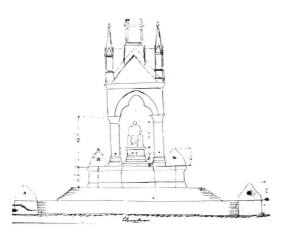

Front elevation

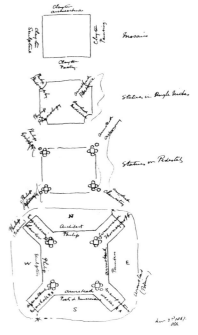

Diagram of platforms

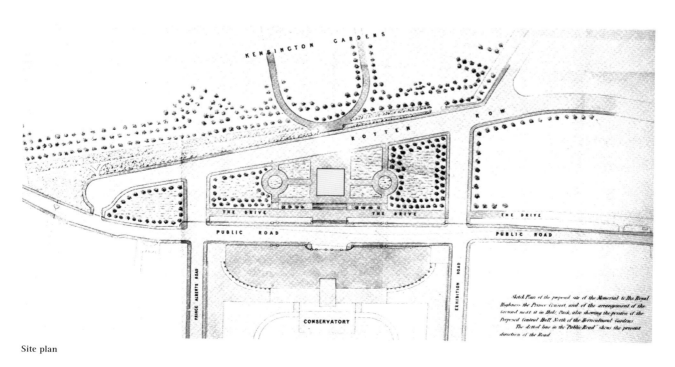

Site plan

Banks

88

The industrial revolution swelled the numbers of the middle class, which in the Victorian era comprised not only wealthy manufacturers but also civil servants, office workers and merchants, all of them essential to the smooth workings of the colossal imperial machine. The emergence of these new capitalists sparked a proliferation of banks, so in the 19th century architects were faced with the challenge of coming up with a design model for the growing number of financial institutions. The monumentality of Victorian architecture was perfectly suited to this type of building, which needed to convey an impression of power, permanence and trustworthiness. The perpetuation of the neoclassical aesthetic was a reflection of the conservatism of the banking world. Paradoxically, the architectural revolution in this field was initiated by one of the firms with the longest history, Lloyd's of London, which commissioned Richard Rogers to design its new headquarters, now recognised as a classic of high-tech architecture.

▲ 11 | BANCA COMMERCIALE ITALIANA
City
1850 *Sancton Wood*
Wood, who had acquired a reputation for designing railway stations, applied the architectural model of the *palazzo* to the main office of this Italian bank. The ground floor opens on to the street via a Tuscan colonnade supporting an arcade, while the other three storeys, characterized by their abundant openings, are crowned by a continuous Italianate cornice that unites the two façades.

▲ 12 | NATIONAL WESTMINSTER BANK
City
1865 *John Gibson*
Gibson, who was responsible for the design of several banks, created a Corinthian pavilion for the former National Provincial Bank. Its single storey is bordered by paired columns which set off several intricately detailed friezes. On the cornice, a series of statues set on each of the columns stands guard over the heavily ornamented building.

▲ 13 | ROYAL BANK OF SCOTLAND
City
1877 *Thomas Chatfield Clarke*
This neoclassical façade made of Portland stone reflects the building's functional layout. On the ground floor, the large windows framed by Ionic columns provide views of the activity in the banking hall, while the offices on the two upper floors are distinguished by Corinthian pilasters flanking the two rows of openings, which are set off by the attic windows on top.

▲ 14 | BANK OF ENGLAND
City
1921 *Herbert Baker*
In 1734 the Bank of England set up shop in the house of one of its founders. This building was later enlarged by Soane between 1788 and 1808 by means of new halls with insuperable handling of space and light. Although these additions disappeared after Baker's refurbishment in the 20th century, the original design was partially restored in 1988 when an area inside the bank was turned into a museum.

▲ 15 | NATIONAL WESTMINSTER BANK, THREADNEEDLE STREET
City
1922 *Mewès and Davis*
Mewès and Davis renounced their habitual French influences for this building with a curved façade and instead sought inspiration in the Renaissance architect Peruzzi, particularly his Palazzo Massimi in Rome. The main entrances flanked by columns bestow distinction on the façade, where the openings become smaller and less ornamented as they approach the attic.

▲ 11

▲ 12

▲ 13

▲ 15

▲ 14

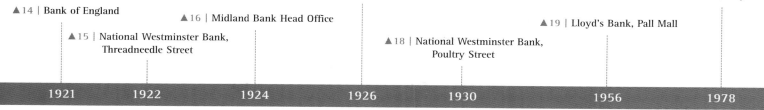

▲16

▲19

▲17

▲16 | MIDLAND BANK HEAD OFFICE
City
1924 *Edwin Lutyens*
Lutyens used his mastery of classicism to endow this building with an elegant and ingenious composition that makes it stand out in the narrow streets of the City. The main façade, six storeys high, features several inset elements that diminish the overall sense of weightiness. The interiors are outstanding examples of classicism, with pride of place being given to marble.

▲17 | BARCLAYS BANK
Westminster
1926 *W. Curtis Green*
On the main façade, a series of massive arches closed off by wrought-iron doors support the Corinthian colonnade running in front of the inset openings of the offices. Although the imposing Barclays building established the template for banks' head offices, it lacks the originality and lightness of the National Westminster Bank in Piccadilly, which Curtis Green completed shortly before.

▲18 | NATIONAL WESTMINSTER BANK, POULTRY STREET
City
1930 *Edwin Cooper*
Faced with the difficulty of appropriately resolving the junction of Prince's St. with Poultry St., Cooper drew on a classical model for this building, which is surrounded by the headquarters of other illustrious banks. The conventional elements are overshadowed by the imposing columns that flank the inset openings on the central storeys and the sculptured ornamentation on the entrance façade.

▲19 | LLOYD'S BANK, PALL MALL
Westminster
1956 *D. Armstrong Smith, Donald McMorran*
The compendium of influences displayed by this cube of Portland stone reflects the desire to abandon rigid classicism after World War II. Its proportions respect neo-Georgian rules, while the inset openings recall the Italian rationalists of the 1930s and the symmetrical pavilions on the terrace roof are inspired by the work of Lutyens.

▲20 | LLOYD'S OF LONDON
City
1978 *Richard Rogers and Partners*
The sculptural originality of the new headquarters of this centuries-old institution caused a great stir. The height of this building with a rectangular base varies from twelve storeys on the north side to six on the south. The placement of the service towers on the exterior made it possible to take full advantage of the space in the interior, centred on a magnificent courtyard 84 m (276 ft) high.

▲18

▲20

Stations

The 19th century witnessed a great expansion of the railway network in London, allowing thousands of people from the outlying residential neighbourhoods to commute to the city every day to work. London Bridge Station, begun in 1836, was the first of six stations to be built within the borders of the City in a mere thirty years. The 1860s were particularly fruitful in this respect, with Victoria, Charing Cross and St. Pancras emerging as standard bearers of the railway boom. The Victorians' dual obsession with state-of-the-art engineering and architectural styles of the past gave rise to colossal train stations in which intricate Gothic detail always went hand in hand with complex multi-level structures that stood out amidst the smog. The elegant glass cannon vault that covered the platforms became the most characteristic feature of Victorian stations, and it has been reproduced, as a form of homage, in more recent stations, such as the Waterloo International Terminal.

▲21

▲23

▲22

▲24

▲25

▲21 | LONDON BRIDGE STATION
Southwark
1836 *George Smith, Samuel Beazley*
Shortly after this station opened, it was enlarged to play host to two different lines. This process left it with one building with a brick and stucco façade and another enormous structure made of glass and cast iron. Unfortunately, the Blitz razed part of this terminal to the ground and nowadays it is necessary to negotiate the large complex that has been put up in the forecourt to see the remains of the original construction.

▲22 | PADDINGTON STATION
Westminster
1850 *I. K. Brunel, M. D. Wyatt, O. Jones*
Apart from the construction of a fourth platform, this station has barely changed since it opened. The Great Western Hotel, designed by P. C. Hardwick, marks the south entrance, which leads on to platforms covered by a vaulted iron-and-glass structure 70 m (230 ft) wide. The terminal contrasts with the modernity of the adjoining offices, drawn up by P. E. Culverhouse in 1933 for the railway company.

▲23 | KING'S CROSS STATION
Camden
1851 *Lewis Cubitt, Joseph Cubitt*
This station, with its subdued Italianate style, is restrained in comparison with its neighbour, St. Pancras ▲28. The main façade is made up of arches that correspond with the two 26 m (85 ft) wide vaulted lobbies, separated by a square central tower 37 m (121 ft) high. The completion of the high-speed train connection with the Continent is has led to modifications in this area.

▲24 | FENCHURCH STREET STATION
City
1853 *George Berkeley*
The construction of this station – the first to be completed in the City – sparked the development of the outlying neighbourhoods of Hackney and Highgate. The main façade – two storeys of brickwork in Italianate style – is crowned by a curved frontispiece that echoes the form of the structure covering the platforms. The distinctive zigzag glass canopy was added in the 1960s.

▲25 | VICTORIA STATION
Westminster
1862 *John Fowler*
Before the two companies that ran this station merged in 1923, each of them had built their own terminals: to the east stand two vaulted structures made of iron and glass, while the construction to the west, set on the Grosvenor Canal, was rebuilt in the early 20th century. The station is adjoined by the Grosvenor Hotel, characterised by its Italianate design crowned by French-style pavilions.

90

▲27

▲28

▲26

▲29

▲30

▲26 | CHARING CROSS STATION
Westminster
1863 *John Hawkshaw*
Like the other Victorian stations, Charing Cross is inseparable from its hotel, designed by Barry in 1865. It takes up the station's ornate northern façade, while to the south stands the majestic form of Embankment Place, the office area that Terry Farrell built above the platforms in 1990. Opposite the station, the pillar by the Eleanor Cross serves as London's zero milestone.

▲27 | CANNON STREET STATION
City
1865 *J. Hawkshaw, E. M. Barry*
The magnificent square towers and brick walls to the east and west are virtually the only original elements to have survived in Cannon Street. The building's roof was dismantled before World War II and replaced in the 1960s by the office complex that John Poulson built above the station, taking with it the façade of Barry's hotel.

▲28 | ST. PANCRAS STATION
Camden
1866 *W. H. Barlow, R. M. Ordish*
The Gothic revival found full expression in both the station and the hotel designed by George Gilbert Scott. This complex, with its intricate interior layout, stood out in the murky 19th-century city for its colourful combination of several different materials. The station and its surroundings are currently being refurbished as part of the project to complete London's rail connection with the Continent.

▲29 | LIVERPOOL STREET STATION
City
1874 *E. Wilson, W. N. Asbee*
One of the last great stations built in London in the 19th century, Liverpool Street reflects the persistence of the neo-Gothic trend, albeit in a much more restrained fashion than in St. Pancras ▲28. Both the station and the hotel annexe were thoroughly overhauled in the 1980s and 1990s as part of the huge project for Broadgate ●10, situated to the west of the main building.

▲30 | WATERLOO INTERNATIONAL TERMINAL
Lambeth
1993 *Nicholas Grimshaw*
The major communications hub of Waterloo, which has been renovated on several occasions, currently contains four train stations and one coach station. To the west of the main building lies the international terminal, with an impressive, 400-m-long (131-ft-long) glass vault that has presided over the arrival of Eurostar trains from the Continent for a decade.

▲30 | Waterloo International Terminal
Nicholas Grimshaw

The major feat of engineering required to connect London with the Continent demanded an impressive station to match. This was brought to life in 1994 with a design that paid homage to the emblematic stations of the Victorian era. Waterloo International Terminal comprises three main elements: an underground concrete parallelepiped (geometric solid) that serves as a base for the station and contains the car park; a two-storey viaduct that supports the platforms and, finally, the colossal steel-and-glass roof that follows the curved trajectory of the five tracks and adapts to the changing width of the platforms. This ductility is achieved through the partial superimposition of conventional panes of glass on to the light, stainless-steel structure. After a decade in operation, the announcement that the enlargement of St. Pancras ▲28 in 2007 would involve a centralization of the Continental connection casts doubt on the future of the spectacular Waterloo Terminal.

DISTRICT Lambeth
LOCATION York Road, SE17
DATE OF CONSTRUCTION 1993

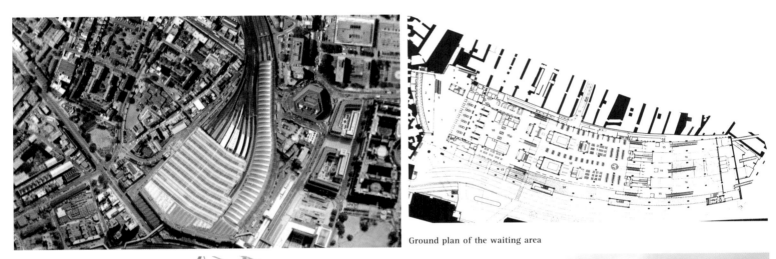

Ground plan of the waiting area

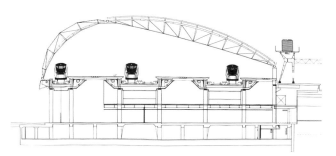

Cross-section

Longitudinal section

Churches

Before the Great Fire of 1666, the City contained nearly one hundred churches within its expanse of barely a square mile. Several monasteries also started to spring up around this nucleus from the 12th century onward; one of these would end up becoming Westminster Abbey ■006, while another, on the other side of the river, would be turned into Southwark Cathedral ■003. Despite the havoc wreaked by the fire, it is still possible to see – at least in part – Norman, Gothic and Palladian churches that bear witness to the city's architectural richness prior to the disaster. Wren was commissioned to rebuild many of the eighty churches that were destroyed, including St. Paul's Cathedral ■028, which was finished in 1711. The new neighbourhoods that grew up over the course of the 18th century fomented the development of religious architecture, giving rise to such significant examples as St. Mary-le-Strand ■041 and St. Martin-in-the-Fields ■044. Despite the destruction caused by World War Two, the City and Westminster still concentrate the greater part of the city's churches, showcasing a wide range of architectural movements.

▲31

▲32

▲33

▲34

▲35

▲31 | ST. MARGARET, WESTMINSTER
Westminster
1120
Despite having been partially rebuilt on several occasions, St. Margaret's, designed in a Gothic and neo-Gothic style, has conserved its original naves, while the tower was renovated in 1735 and the apse is the result of an enlargement undertaken in 1758. The proximity of St. Margaret's to Westminster has made it the official parish church of the House of Commons.

▲32 | TEMPLE CHURCH
City
1185
One of the earliest examples of London's Gothic architecture, Temple Church was extensively restored in the 19th century. Its distinctive circular nave, 18 m (59 ft) in diameter, is inspired by the Church of the Holy Sepulchre in Jerusalem. Other notable features include the beautiful marble columns in the clerestory and the presbytery, as well as the latter's pointed openings dating from the 13th-century enlargement.

▲33 | HENRY VII'S CHAPEL
Westminster
1512
The perpendicular late Gothic style bestows a special majesty on this building in Westminster Abbey ■006. The ornamentation on the columns and buttresses alleviates its structural weight, while the interior is dominated by the pillars that support the fan vault and define the nave. The large pointed openings allow light to pour on to the rich decoration, complete with original statues.

▲34 | ST. PAUL, COVENT GARDEN
Westminster
1631 *Inigo Jones*
The monumental Tuscan portico of this Etruscan temple provides shelter to passersby on the western side of the piazza, while the entrance is set in the rear façade. This church is distinguished by the ample eaves and frontispieces with jutting wooden beams. After a devastating fire in 1795, Thomas Hardwick restored the building, eliminating the side galleries in the process.

▲35 | ST. VEDAST-ALIAS-FOSTER
City
1670 *Christopher Wren*
The tower is the outstanding element in this simple church, where the main volume is a parallelepiped with a flat roof. The bell tower is square at ground level but narrows above the cornice to display a baroque combination of transparencies and both concave and convex forms, crowned by a weather vane on the pinnacle.

92

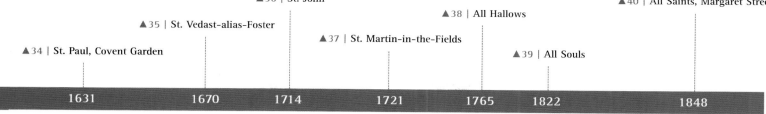

▲34 | St. Paul, Covent Garden   ▲35 | St. Vedast-alias-Foster   ▲36 | St. John   ▲37 | St. Martin-in-the-Fields   ▲38 | All Hallows   ▲39 | All Souls   ▲40 | All Saints, Margaret Street

1631   1670   1714   1721   1765   1822   1848

▲36   ▲37

▲40

▲38   ▲39

▲36 | ST. JOHN
Westminster
1714 *Thomas Archer*

This example of English baroque is marked out on its four corners by square towers topped with a lantern. On the north and south façades, majestic Tuscan porticos provide access to the church, while the large Venetian windows of the east and west elevations allow light to pour inside. This church, which was rebuilt after the bombardments, is now used as a concert hall.

▲37 | ST. MARTIN-IN-THE-FIELDS
Westminster
1721 *James Gibbs*

This baroque church in the northwest corner of Trafalgar Square ●21 offers a resting place for pedestrians on the steps of its slender portico. The frontispiece backs on to a square tower crowned with an elaborate pinnacle. The building's isolated position makes it possible to appreciate the monumentality of its other three façades, characterised by their generous openings.

▲38 | ALL HALLOWS
City
1765 *George Dance the Younger*

The dense network of streets that once surrounded this church of medieval origin has disappeared over the course of time to reveal the full austerity of its brick walls. The square tower with a dome on top provides access to a splendid interior, in which columns partially embedded in the walls support the cannon vault and six semicircular windows opening on to the frieze illuminate this beautiful coffering.

▲39 | ALL SOULS
Westminster
1822 *John Nash*

The originality of this church – designed by Nash to finish off the northern end of Regent Street – lies in its portico, which is circular and is topped by a Corinthian peristyle supporting an eye-catching conical pinnacle. This design caused great controversy in its day. The church's interior consists of a rectangular nave with a flat coffered roof inspired by Wren.

▲40 | ALL SAINTS, MARGARET STREET
Westminster
1848 *William Butterfield*

This neo-Gothic church, one of most outstanding examples of Victorian religious architecture, is set to the rear of a small courtyard framed by its rectory and choir school. The entrance on the south façade is dominated by a slender slate tower culminating in a steeple, while the profusely decorated interior inspired the members of the Arts and Crafts Movement.

Museums

Many art connoisseurs donated their precious collections to the State in the 18th and 19th centuries in order to demonstrate every aspect of the world's diversity to the public. This didactic zeal, which would reach its apogee in the Victorian era, fomented the emergence of London's great museums in the 19th century. Although the first public art gallery was completed in 1814, the major museums opened in the 1830s and 1840s, when neoclassicism determined the aesthetic approach of the British Museum and the Imperial War Museum, among others. In the second half of the century, the neo-Gothic movement made an impact on the main temples of culture, as evidenced by the ornamented façade of the Natural History Museum. Once London had recovered from the wars of the 20th century, it threw in its lot with the latest architectural trends, with extremely controversial results like the Museum of London. The museums that have opened in recent decades reflect the eclecticism of the modern world, with starting points as wide-ranging as international architectural movements and the rehabilitation of old industrial spaces.

94

▲ 41

▲ 42

▲ 44

▲ 43

▲ 45

▲ 41 | NATIONAL GALLERY
Westminster
1838 *William Wilkins*
The long main façade of this museum to the north of Trafalgar Square ●21 comprises a central portico built with the former columns of Carlton House ■069, plus six sections on each side. The portico leads to a dome, framed by two pavilions on either side. The interior was chiefly designed by Edward Middleton Barry, while the lobby is the work of John Taylor.

▲ 42 | IMPERIAL WAR MUSEUM
Southwark
1839 *J. Lewis, S. Smirke, Arup Associates*
In 1838 Smirke endowed this old hospital with an additional central portico and dome, while the east and west wings were demolished to make way for the surrounding park. The original courtyard was taken over in 1989 by the extension drawn up by Arup and Associates, which consists of four floors of galleries set around a large lobby with a glass-roofed vault.

▲ 43 | VICTORIA AND ALBERT MUSEUM
Kensington
1856 *F. Fowke, G. Sykes, A. Webb*
This museum of the decorative arts promoted by Prince Albert has grown over the years. Particularly worthy of note in the later extensions – which are fully integrated into the surrounding terracotta, brick and mosaic of Kensington – are the arched gallery designed by Sykes, Webb's opulent east and west façades and the interiors clad with ceramics in the New Refreshment Room and the Grill Room.

▲ 44 | NATURAL HISTORY MUSEUM
Westminster
1881 *Alfred Waterhouse*
The museum's main façade is over 200 m (656 ft) long and its ornamentation, based on various zoological motifs carved in stone, dominates Cromwell Road. The main entrance, flanked by two square towers 60 m (197 ft) high, leads on to a huge lobby notable for its monumental staircase and its roof of steel and glass.

▲ 45 | HORNIMAN MUSEUM
Lewisham
1896 *C. H. Townsend, Allies and Morrison*
This museum, considered to be Townsend's masterpiece, displays an asymmetrical composition dominated by a side tower with a circular cornice. The main façade has no openings but is decorated with a large mosaic by Anning Bell, which contrasts with the simplicity and functionality of the interiors. An extension in 2002 added a new block, which drew inspiration from Townsend's original project.

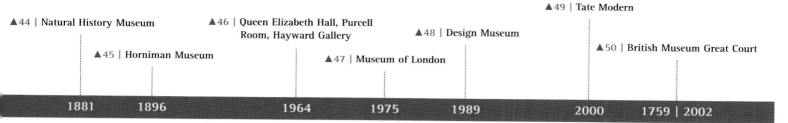

▲44 | Natural History Museum

▲46 | Queen Elizabeth Hall, Purcell Room, Hayward Gallery

▲49 | Tate Modern

▲48 | Design Museum

▲45 | Horniman Museum

▲50 | British Museum Great Court

▲47 | Museum of London

1881   1896   1964   1975   1989   2000   1759 | 2002

▲48

▲47

▲49

▲46

▲50

▲46 | QUEEN ELIZABETH HALL, PURCELL ROOM, HAYWARD GALLERY

Lambeth

1964 *LCC/GLC Architects Department, Hubert Bennet, Jack Whittle*

These imposing concrete buildings, inspired by Brutalism, are linked by elevated bridges that allow visitors to stroll around the exterior of the complex. The Queen Elizabeth Hall and Purcell Room, with a seating capacity of 917 and 370 respectively, share the same foyer, while the Hayward Gallery puts on exhibitions organised by the Arts Council in its five galleries.

▲47 | MUSEUM OF LONDON

City

1975 *Powell and Moya*

This example of 1960s' utilitarian architecture contains a formidable collection related to the history of the city. A high walkway connects the entrance to the museum with street level, although the refurbishment project due to be undertaken by Wilkinson Eyre in 2009 will provide the building with a new entrance and a greater number of exhibition rooms.

▲48 | DESIGN MUSEUM

Southwark

1989 *Conran Roche*

This white stucco museum with clear-cut lines, built as part of the conversion project for Butler's Wharf ●57, draws heavily on the international architecture of the 1930s. An old dockside warehouse of little architectural value provided the starting point for this building, endowed with three floors that open on to the view of the river by means of various terraces.

▲49 | TATE MODERN

Southwark

2000 *Herzog and De Meuron*

The Tate Modern, one of the four Tate galleries scattered over England, displays an extraordinary collection of international modern art. Set in the mythical Bankside Power Station ■103 designed by Giles Gilbert Scott, which had been out of service since 1982, this museum has become one of the stars of the regeneration project on the south bank of the Thames.

▲50 | BRITISH MUSEUM GREAT COURT

Camden

1759, 2002 *Foster and Partners*

This project reinvented the circular courtyard of the British Museum ■067. This area had once housed a library inside a central cylinder. The museum's new circulation system revolves around this volume, which has been refurbished and surrounded by staircases that connect the ground floor with the upper galleries. The courtyard is protected by a glass roof with a striking geometrical form, designed to take maximum advantage of natural light.

95

▲50 | British Museum Great Court
Foster and Partners

In 1857, the old garden in this central area was closed to the public to build a library on the site. This addition made it difficult to move from one part of the museum to another, but this problem was rectified at the end of the 20th century when the book collection was transferred to the library in St. Pancras. As a result, the courtyard could be converted into an excellent circulation space endowed with new entrances to the galleries. This made it possible to walk round the ground floor without interruptions for the first time in 150 years. The old reading room, now an information centre and specialised library, is covered all round its perimeter by a stone cladding that hides the pillars supporting the glass structure designed to protect the Great Court. A new portico was also built on the south side to house the lifts and connect the bright central space with the front patio, which was similarly refurbished by Foster.

DISTRICT Camden
LOCATION Great Russell Street, WC1
DATE OF CONSTRUCTION 1759, 2002

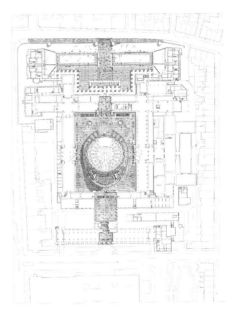

Location plan

95B

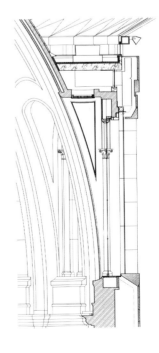

Detailed section

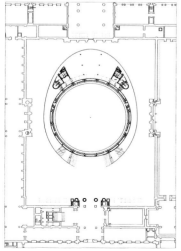

Ground Floor

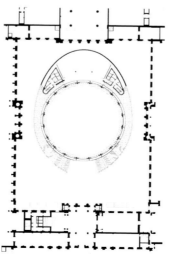

First Floor

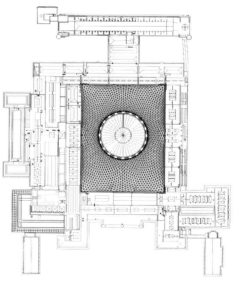

Plan of the roofs

Palaces

Ever since the construction of the Tower of London ■002, the city has played host to numerous palaces built to house royalty, aristocrats and clergymen. By the Middle Ages, the City could already boast a number of palatial residences that accommodated nobles from all over England when they visited the capital. In the 16th century the aristocracy took advantage of Henry VIII's confiscation of Church land to put up their palaces. Henry himself supervised the construction of several royal residences, such as Whitehall, Richmond and Windsor. In the 17th century, the unsanitary conditions in the City prompted the gentry to seek refuge in rural areas, leading to the development of St. James's Palace ▲55, Hampton Court ▲54 and Greenwich. This trend was reversed in the Georgian era, as the prevailing economic prosperity enabled aristocrats living in the country to build new urban palaces. The last big investments in this field came at the end of this era, with the renovations of Kew Palace and Buckingham Palace ■066.

▲ 51

▲ 52

▲ 53

▲ 55

▲ 54

▲ 51 | LAMBETH PALACE
Lambeth
1297
This medieval, Tudor and Jacobean palace is separated from the river by the Albert Embankment. The main entrance is marked by two five-storey towers flanking two arches – one for vehicles and the other for pedestrians. The most outstanding building in the complex is the Great Hall, to the south of the cloisters that form part of the neo-Jacobean enlargement undertaken in the early 19th century.

▲ 52 | BISHOP'S PALACE, FULHAM
Hammersmith
1420
This old bishopric, closer to a country house than a palace, integrates various architectural styles. The courtyard – clad with brickwork decorated with a repeated ornamental motif in black – dates from 1520. In contrast, the bell tower was built in the 18th century, while the chapel, an addition from the second half of the 19th century, is remarkable for the Gothic style of its polychrome walls.

▲ 53 | ELTHAM PALACE
Greenwich
1479
The most notable feature of this old royal palace is the magnificent hall, with large windows that cast light on the ceiling with hammer beams. When the palace was abandoned after the Civil War, this room was subsequently used as a barn, before being restored in the 20th century. The rest of the building has barely been preserved, although an interesting combination of architectural styles is seen in the courtyard.

▲ 54 | HAMPTON COURT PALACE
Outer West
1514 *Christopher Wren, William Kent*
Several monarchs undertook the task of converting this Tudor mansion into a classical palace, and as a consequence it presents a good sample of various architectural movements. The splendid redbrick Gothic façade to the west leads to a series of courtyards from different eras, decorated with exquisite flourishes like Renaissance terracotta medallions and a classical colonnade made of Portland stone.

▲ 55 | ST. JAMES'S PALACE
Westminster
1530
This old royal residence, commissioned by Henry VIII, was originally arranged around four courtyards, but these were destroyed by a fire in 1809 and then by subsequent rebuilding. However, it is still possible to see the original north façade, with its Tudor battlements and turrets, and the royal chambers on the south elevation, attributed to Wren.

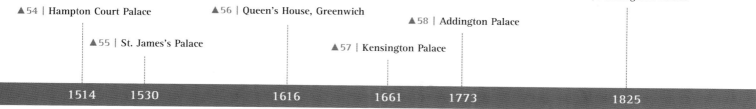

▲ 56

▲ 56 | QUEEN'S HOUSE, GREENWICH
Greenwich
1616 *Inigo Jones*

Jones designed this residence for Queen Anne with two parallel buildings, linked by a bridge on the first floor. His Palladian project is notable for its strict classical proportions, the Ionic lodge on the south façade and the curvilinear symmetry of the staircases leading to the north terrace. The interior, restored in 1990, is a perfect match for the classical exterior.

▲ 57

▲ 57 | KENSINGTON PALACE
Kensington
1661 *Christopher Wren, Nicholas Hawksmoor, William Kent, Thomas Ripley (attributed)*

This royal residence represents the sum of various enlargements arranged in a disorderly fashion around three courtyards. Wren contributed the south and east façades, along with royal chambers designed on a domestic scale. Hawksmoor drew up the Orangery, a brick building with an austere white interior. Finally, George I added new courtyards to endow the palace with a more regal air.

▲ 58

▲ 58 | ADDINGTON PALACE
Croydon
1773 *Robert Mylne*

This Palladian mansion, which served as a bishopric in the 19th century, originally comprised two floors plus a loft. Single-storey wings extended outward to the north and south, but in 1848 these were enlarged and aligned with the rest of the building. Norman Shaw refurbished the palace at the turn of the 20th century in an attempt to recapture the original proportions, adding a new storey to the central block in the process.

▲ 59

▲ 59 | BUCKINGHAM PALACE
Westminster
1825 *John Nash, Edward Blore, Aston Webb*

George IV instigated the transformation of this country house into a majestic royal palace, but Nash failed to achieve the degree of opulence required by the king. The palace's west façade has remained unaltered ever since, but the forecourt on the opposite side was turned into new living quarters by Blore. Webb changed the latter façade for a neoclassical pastiche in order to match the splendour of the Mall ● 15.

Bridges

The Thames is London's *raison d'être* and its bridges form an inextricable part of the city's identity. The only means of crossing the river until the 18th century was provided by London Bridge, the Roman bridge that was rebuilt on various occasions. Despite the protests of boatmen and traders who had shops on this path across the river, in 1747 Westminster Bridge ▲60 was opened to link the seat of government, to the west, with Lambeth, to the east. Two decades later, the development of Southwark was boosted by the construction of Blackfriars Bridge ▲62, which connects the City with the south bank. The technological advances of the Victorian era led to infrastructural improvements propitiated by the construction of embankments and bridges, such as Albert Bridge ▲63 and Chelsea Bridge ▲67, and viaducts with railway lines, such as Hungerford Bridge ▲61. The expansion of the city over the course of the 19th and 20th centuries, coupled with the increasing density of its population, made it necessary to build new bridges – the last being a product of the 21st century, the pedestrian Millennium Bridge ▲69.

98

▲60

▲61   ▲62

▲63   ▲64

▲60 | WESTMINSTER BRIDGE

Westminster-Lambeth
1862 *Thomas Page*
Today's bridge, built a couple of years before the development of the Victoria Embankment, replaced an old viaduct dating from 1747. With its seven arches spread along its length and its imposing width, the bridge is embellished with ornamental details designed by Charles Barry, the architect of the nearby Houses of Parliament ■075. Westminster Bridge connects the latter with County Hall, on the south bank.

▲61 | HUNGERFORD BRIDGE

Westminster-Lambeth
1863 *John Hawkshaw, Lifschutz Davidson Sandilands*
This is the only bridge in the centre of London that serves both pedestrians and trains. The tracks leading to the terminal of Charing Cross ▲26 occupy the central stretch, while Hawkshaw's original walkways that ran alongside the distinctive iron trusses on either side of the rails were replaced in 2002 by light cable-stayed bridges made of steel and concrete.

▲62 | BLACKFRIARS BRIDGE

City-Southwark
1869 *James Cubitt*
In 1769 Robert Mylne completed an Italianate viaduct that would enhance the development of Southwark. A century later, this construction was replaced by a new bridge with five wrought-iron arches designed to bear both road vehicles and pedestrians. Meanwhile, Cubitt took charge of the construction of a railway bridge that was put up a few yards down river.

▲63 | ALBERT BRIDGE

Kensington-Wandsworth
1873 *Rouwland Mason Ordish*
This bridge, which spans the 216 m (709 ft) separating Chelsea from Battersea, represents a great feat of Victorian engineering, dating from the same period as the Chelsea Embankment. The first partially suspended viaduct over the Thames was originally held up by four towers 21 m (69 ft) high, which were reinforced in 1973 by the addition of central pillars.

▲64 | TOWER BRIDGE

Tower Hamlets-Southwark
1886 *J. Wolfe Barry, Horace Jones*
This bridge, one of London's most famous postcard images, comprises a steel structure clad with granite and Portland stone. Two passageways stretch between the two towers built in a neo-Gothic style; one opens to allow ships to pass through, while the higher one is designed for pedestrian use.

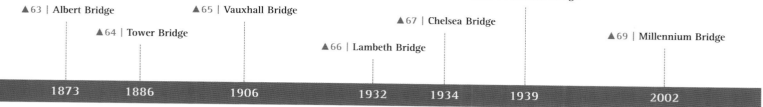

▲65   ▲66

▲65 | VAUXHALL BRIDGE

Westminster-Lambeth

1906 *Maurice Fitzmaurice, W. E. Riley*

This steel bridge with five arches, measuring over 245 m (804 ft) long, is particularly notable for the sculptures that adorn its granite supporting pillars. These figures, which represent the arts and sciences, include an effigy of Architecture bearing a model of St. Paul's Cathedral ■028 in her arms.

▲66 | LAMBETH BRIDGE

Westminster-Lambeth

1932 *LCC Architects Department, G. Topham Forrest, Reginald Blomfield*

This construction, made up of five arches rising from brickwork bases, replaced a suspension bridge that had been opened in 1862. Each of the bases is decorated with a pair of obelisks, with particularly large ones at each end of the span. Lambeth Bridge forms part of the monumental ensemble designed to connect Thames House – to the north – with the gardens on the Embankment to the south.

99

▲67

▲67 | CHELSEA BRIDGE

Kensington-Wandsworth

1934 *G. Topham Forrest, E. P. Wheeler*

This 107-m-long (351-ft-long) suspension bridge replaced a similar construction that had been completed in 1858. Its northern end, next to the Royal Chelsea Hospital, marks the frontier between Pimlico and Chelsea, while its southern end opens up next to Battersea Park ●58. The steel structure looks particularly impressive when seen with the bridge's spectacular night-time illumination.

▲68

▲68 | WATERLOO BRIDGE

Westminster-Lambeth

1939 *Giles Gilbert Scott*

London's first concrete bridge was only completed with great difficulty, on account of the outbreak of World War II during the construction process. It comprises five low arches clad in Portland stone and was built to replace another structure dating from the early 19th century. Both the ornamentation and the access areas were designed with great elegance and attention to detail.

▲69

▲69 | MILLENNIUM BRIDGE

City-Southwark

2002 *Norman Foster, Anthony Caro, Arup Associates*

This 320-m-long (1,050-ft-long) bridge, once described as a scythe of light over the river, was the first pedestrian bridge to be built over the river in over a century. This great feat of engineering and design – made up of two Y-shape bases supporting an aluminium walkway – provides a convenient link between the City and Southwark.

▲69 | Millennium Bridge
Norman Foster, Anthony Caro, Arup Associates

This bridge – the fruit of the joint efforts of an architect (Foster), an engineering firm (Arup) and a sculptor (Caro) – has redrawn the map of London for pedestrians. Two Y-shape steel-and-concrete pillars are embedded in the river to support the eight tensed cables that flank the 4-m-wide (13-ft-wide) platform, which in its turn rests on steel crossbars, placed at intervals of 8 m (26 ft) and attached to the longitudinal cables. The innovative lateral suspension of this ingenious structure eliminated the need to construct the high pillars required by the other suspension bridges on the Thames. It was opened in 2000, but the massive influx of visitors in the following days gave rise to unexpected swaying. This made it necessary to close the bridge, which reopened two years later after being equipped with shock absorbers that regulate the effect of pedestrians' footsteps.

DISTRICT Westminster-Lambeth
LOCATION Bankside, the City
DATE OF CONSTRUCTION 2002

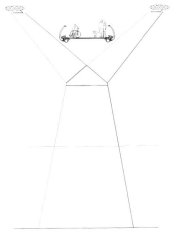

Cross-section

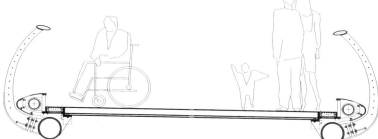

Detail of the section of the walkway

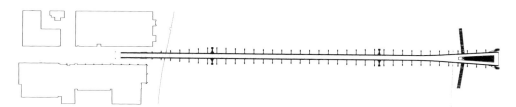

Ground plan

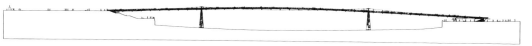

Longitudinal section

Hotels

London lacked big hotels until the 19th century, as prior to that travellers stayed in small boarding houses or, if they were wealthier, in their own city residences. The development of the railway that began in the 1830s caused an upsurge in travelling and so gave rise to a need for bigger hotels, which were adopted by the railway companies themselves as a symbol of their prosperity. A new institution emerged alongside the city's main stations: the grand hotel. This went on to become the type of building that best reflected the aspirations of Victorian society. The following decades witnessed the appearance of exclusive establishments like the Savoy and the Ritz, which served as meeting places for aristocrats and well-to-do members of the middle class. The ostentation of the neo-Gothic style, the restrained luxury of the Edwardian era and the solidity of Art Deco gave way, after World War II, to a controversial quest for modernity, manifested by skyscrapers like the London Hilton. In recent years, the renovated areas of the East End and the South Bank have opened their first hotels.

▲70

▲71

▲72

▲73

▲74

▲70 | GREAT EASTERN HOTEL

City

1884 *Charles Barry*

This big redbrick Victorian hotel was set alongside Liverpool Street Station ▲29, one of the last great railway terminals to be built in the city. The neo-Gothic façade – with its sloping attics and outsize chimneys perfectly preserved – conceals interiors that were refurbished in 2000 to combine some of the original features with a more cutting-edge look.

▲71 | SAVOY HOTEL

Westminster

1889 *Arthur Mackmurdo, Thomas Collcutt*

This emblematic hotel is built in two parts, one alongside the Strand and the other next to the river. The former, designed by Collcutt, reflects his eclectic style, although its unity is ensured by the use of white terracotta cladding. Mackmurdo's section, which contains the bedrooms, resembles the commercial architecture of the Chicago School. The hotel's legendary entrance was refurbished in Art-Deco style in 1929.

▲72 | RUSSELL HOTEL

Camden

1898 *C. Fitzroy Doll*

This splendid hotel, an example of late Victorian architecture, was the first large-scale building to be built in Georgian Bloomsbury. The nine-storey building bears the stamp of the eclecticism characteristic of the period, particularly in the ornamented elevations crowned by octagonal pavilions at each end.

▲73 | CONNAUGHT HOTEL

Westminster

1901 *Isaacs and Florence*

The Connaught stands on Mount Street, a sophisticated street characterised by the reddish terracotta cladding of its ornamented façades. This opulent hotel has barely changed since it first opened as an exclusive haunt for wealthy travellers. Its classical portico leads on to a majestic entrance lobby, embellished by a superb mosaic floor and a caoba-wood staircase.

▲74 | PICCADILLY HOTEL

Westminster

1905 *R. Norman Shaw*

Shaw's last great building in the Edwardian baroque style was also the only part of his plan for the urban development of Piccadilly Circus that saw the light of day. The main façade, topped by a sloping attic and an elaborate frontispiece at the western end, is distinguished by the three-storey Ionic colonnade that protects the bedrooms, which are set back from the noise of the street.

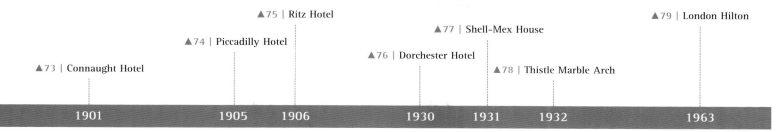
▲73 | Connaught Hotel
▲74 | Piccadilly Hotel
▲75 | Ritz Hotel
▲76 | Dorchester Hotel
▲77 | Shell-Mex House
▲78 | Thistle Marble Arch
▲79 | London Hilton

1901   1905   1906   1930   1931   1932   1963

▲75

▲79

▲77

▲78

▲76

101

▲75 | RITZ HOTEL

Westminster

1906 *Mewès and Davis*

This elegant Edwardian hotel, a contemporary of the Piccadilly Hotel ▲74, was inspired by French architecture for its remarkable two-storey attic and the beautiful arcade of the façade on Piccadilly. Its steel structure, unprecedented in London at the time, is clad with Norwegian granite on the ground floor and Portland stone on the other elevations.

▲76 | DORCHESTER HOTEL

Westminster

1930 *W. Curtis Green*

This hotel, built close to one of the most elegant parts of Hyde Park ●13, was originally drawn up by Owen Williams but he abandoned the project in the face of the difficulties involved in bringing his innovative ideas to life. Curtis Green, who was also responsible for the interior design of some of the rooms, completed the Art-Deco building with a reinforced-concrete structure and an entrance marked by the concavity of its south façade.

▲77 | SHELL-MEX HOUSE

Westminster

1931 *Messrs Joseph*

Originally opened in 1886 as the Cecil Hotel, Shell-Mex House was purchased in 1930 by the eponymous oil company, which commissioned the Joseph firm to renovate the building in an Art Deco style. The austere, 13-storey south elevation, set progressively further back on the upper floors, is crowned by an enormous clock that makes the building instantly recognisable from the north bank of the Thames.

▲78 | THISTLE MARBLE ARCH

Westminster

1932 *John Burnet, Tait and Partners*

As the shop windows running along the bottom of its south façade indicate, the old Mount Royal Hotel stands in the heart of the Oxford Street shopping area. Despite taking up an entire block, the building merges into its surroundings on account of its simple linearity, a testimony of the influence of Dutch architecture and Erich Mendelsohn.

▲79 | LONDON HILTON

Westminster

1963 *Lewis Solomon Kaye*

The 100-m-high (328-ft-high) London Hilton was one of the first skyscrapers to be built in the city. Set on a glass base, the building is spread over three volumes arranged around a central core. Its position close to Hyde Park Corner and the lowness of the buildings surrounding it mean that this tower has become an outstanding feature of the urban landscape.

Theatres

Before the first theatres opened at the end of the 16th century, the performance of dramatic works was confined to the courtyards of inns and the homes of the gentry. The opening of the Rose in 1587 sparked the emergence of competitors such as the Globe ▲80, in 1599, and the Hope, in 1613, but the association of theatre with other more ignoble activities led to a prohibition under the Puritans that lasted until the restoration of the monarchy in 1660. The gradual relaxation of the restrictions affecting the theatre allowed it to acquire a following among the wealthier sections of society over the course of the 18th century. The neoclassical influence was extremely evident in the design of the new playhouses that proliferated in the 19th century. Shaftesbury Avenue became the hub of London's commercial theatre, while less mainstream fare is available on the South Bank – the home of the Royal National Theatre ▲87 – and in fringe theatres outside the West End.

▲80

▲81

▲82

▲83

▲84

▲80 | GLOBE THEATRE
Southwark
1600
The Globe was built on Bankside by Richard Burbage and his company of actors as an open, octagonal amphitheatre with three storeys and a capacity of 3,000 people. After suffering damage from a fire in 1613, it was rebuilt and continued to operate until its closure and subsequent demolition in 1644. In 1997 a faithful reconstruction of the Elizabethan Globe was unveiled close to its original foundation stones.

▲81 | THEATRE ROYAL, DRURY LANE
Westminster
1810 *Benjamin Wyatt, James Spiller, Samuel Beazley*
The Theatre Royal was the victim of several fires and was rebuilt no less than four times on this site to the southeast of Covent Garden. Wyatt's building is endowed with an elegant foyer with elegant staircases leading up to the vaulted circle. Spiller added the portico with Doric pillars in 1820, while Beazley contributed the Ionic colonnade on the east façade.

▲82 | THEATRE ROYAL
Westminster
1831 *John Nash*
Along with the houses on nearby Suffolk Street, the Theatre Royal forms part of the triumphal way planned to run between Carlton House Terrace ■ 069 and Regent's Park ●19. The theatre's main façade has preserved the magnificent portico with six Corinthian pillars, which stand in front of a row of nine circular windows that repeat the design of the central opening on the frontispiece.

▲83 | ROYAL OPERA HOUSE
Westminster
1857 *E. M. Barry, Gollins Melvin Ward Partnership*
Barry's Royal Opera House – which replaced a theatre designed by Smirke that burned down in 1856 – is remarkable for its enormous classical portico with six Corinthian columns standing on a base of dressed stone. In the late 20th century, an ambitious refurbishment project by Dixon Jones modernised and enlarged the theatre by incorporating the adjoining Floral Hall into the complex.

▲84 | ROYAL ALBERT HALL
Westminster
1867 *Captain Francis Fowke*
This legendary auditorium with a capacity of 8,000 people is set in an imposing brick cylinder nearly 91 m (300 ft) in diameter. An impressive terracotta frieze depicting the triumph of the arts and letters runs around the entire perimeter of the building, which is crowned by a glass vault with an iron structure.

02

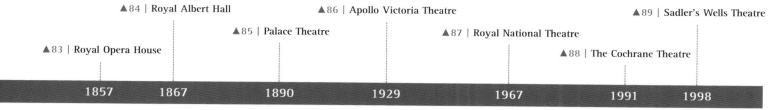

▲84 | Royal Albert Hall   ▲86 | Apollo Victoria Theatre   ▲89 | Sadler's Wells Theatre

▲85 | Palace Theatre   ▲87 | Royal National Theatre

▲83 | Royal Opera House   ▲88 | The Cochrane Theatre

1857   1867   1890   1929   1967   1991   1998

▲85

▲87

▲88

▲86

▲89

▲85 | PALACE THEATRE

Westminster

1890 *Thomas Collcutt*

Collcutt's eclectic style resulted in a building that dominates the west side of Cambridge Circus, in the heart of the West End. Striking linear compositions in shades of red and cream decorate the main façade, which culminates in a frontispiece adorned with various sculptures and flanked by two pavilions.

▲86 | APOLLO VICTORIA THEATRE

Westminster

1929 *E. Walmsley Lewis*

The old New Victoria Cinema was converted into a theatre for musicals in 1981, after remaining closed for six years. The building, which is influenced by the Continental architecture of the 1920s, sports two identical façades with an orderly horizontal composition of parallel rows of windows and parapets that contrasts with the vertical lines of the entrances.

▲87 | ROYAL NATIONAL THEATRE

Lambeth

1967 *Denys Lasdun and Partners*

The extraordinary forms of this building set at the south end of Waterloo Bridge ▲68 resemble a concrete ocean liner docked alongside the river bank. The complex contains three auditoriums – the Olivier, the Lyttelton and the Cottesloe – as well as a foyer with a complex combination of levels and terraces that emphasize the horizontality of the construction.

▲88 | THE COCHRANE THEATRE

Camden

1991 *Robinson Thorne Architects*

The renovation project for this theatre, originally founded in 1964, gathered together within a single space the chaotic group of underused settings on the first floor by creating a foyer with a bar that opened on to the street by means of a projecting glass volume. In addition, the structural elements that remained intact were painted in bright colours to endow them with a sculptural dimension.

▲89 | SADLER'S WELLS THEATRE

Islington

1998 *RHWL Architects, Nicholas Hare Architects*

This theatre with over 300 years of history was refurbished as a result of the fundraising programme of the National Lottery. Apart from rebuilding the auditorium and the stage, the renovation emphasised the contrast between the opacity of the brick walls shrouding much of the building and the transparency of the magnificent three-storey glass foyer.

103

▲87 | Royal National Theatre
Denys Lasdun and Partners

Ever since its construction, this example of English Brutalism has attracted both effusive praise and fierce criticism. On the one hand, it has been argued that its structure based on horizontal strips seeks integration into the riverside setting by rising from the water like a natural bank; on the other, the building was compared by the Prince of Wales to a nuclear power station in the heart of the city. In any case, public opinion seems to be united in its appreciation of the interior, where the centre's cultural offerings are spread across three auditoriums. The Olivier, with a capacity of 1,160, boasts a large open stage inspired by classical Greek theatres; the 890-seater Lyttelton has a conventional proscenium arch and, finally, the Cottesloe, designed for experimental work, consists of a flexible space with mobile banks of seating that can be reached via a separate entrance to the rear of the building.

DISTRICT Lambeth
LOCATION Belvedere Road, South Bank, SE1
DATE OF CONSTRUCTION 1967

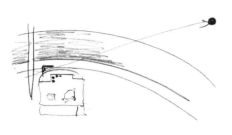

Preliminary sketch

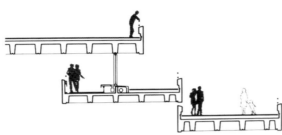

Detail of the section of the terraces

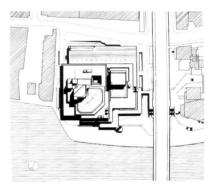

Location plan

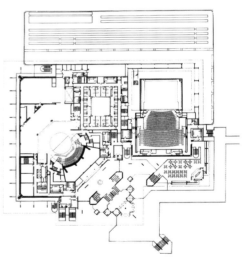

Ground floor

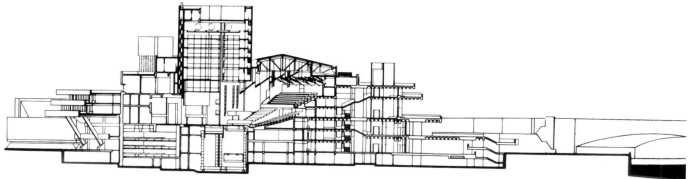

Longitudinal section

BIBLIOGRAPHY

Ackroyd, Peter
London: The Biography
Vintage
2002

Anderson, Robert
The Great Court and the British Museum
British Museum Press
2000

116

Bayley, Stephen
The Albert Memorial: the monument in its social and architectural context
Scolar Press
1981

Butler, Marianne
London Architecture
Metro Publications
2004

Cooke, Sir Robert
The Place of Westminster: Houses of Parliament
Burton Skira
1987

Curtis, William J. R.
Denys Lasdun Architecture, City, Landscape
Phaidon
1994

Doré, Gustave; Jerrold Blanchard
Londres: una peregrinación
Abada Editores
2004

Downes, Kerry
Sir Christopher Wren: the design of St. Paul's Cathedral
1988

Hardingham, Samantha
London: a guide to recent architecture
Batsford
1996

Hart, Vaughan
St. Paul's Cathedral: Sir Christopher Wren
Phaidon
1995

Hibbert, Christopher
London, The biography of a city
Penguin Books
1980

Hibbert, Christopher
The Story of England
Phaidon
2004

Inwood, Stephen
A History of London
New York University Press
2002

Jones, Edward; Woodward, Christopher
A Guide to the Architecture of London
Phoenix Illustrated
1997

Foster, Norman
Norman Foster and the British Museum
Prestel
2001

Friedman, Terry
James Gibbs
Yale University Press
1984

Moore, Rowan
Structure, Space and Skin: the work of Nicholas Grimshaw and Partners
Phaidon
1993

Peacock, John
The Stage Designs of Inigo Jones: the European context
Cambridge University Press
1995

Port, M. H.
The Houses of Parliament
Yale University Press
1976

Sutcliffe, Anthony
London: an architectural history
Yale University Press
2006

Tournier, Paul
Londres: las claves de su historia
Robinbook
2001

CREDITS FOR PHOTOGRAPHS AND ILLUSTRATIONS

All the photographs from the present day:

© Inge Clemente
www.ingeclemente.com

Except:

Page.
19A © Album | akg-images
35B © Nigel Young | Foster and Partners
59   © Zaber Ahmed (Bloomsbury Square)
91A © Album | akg-images
95A © Nigel Young | Foster and Partners
95B © Nigel Young | Foster and Partners

All the illustrations and historical images:

© Album | akg-images

General maps:

© Pilar Cano

Maps of historical evolution:

© Montse Montero

Historical images:

Page 6   *The Tower*. Steel print. Artist unknown.

Page 7   Tower Bridge. Woodprint. Artist unknown.

Page 8   Victoria Embankment. Photograph. Photographer unknown.

Page 14   Plan of the Tower of London. Watercolour. Artist unknown.
          Coronation of William the Conqueror. Jean de Wavrin.
          Marriage of Henry VI with Margaret of Anjou. Print.
          Charles Grignion.

Page 15   *Map of London*. Watercolour. Artist unknown.

Page 16   View of London in 1616. Copper print. Jan Claesz Visscher.
          Inigo Jones. Oil. Kart Barth.

Page 17   *Execution of Charles I*. Etching. Jan Luyken.
          Great Fire of London. Coloured etching. H. Ludolff.
          Christopher Wren. Print. Alexander Bannerman.

Page 18   *Triumphant entrance into London of William III*. Artist unknown.

Page 20   *Portrait of George III of Hanover*. Oil on canvas. Artist unknown.
          Guildhall. Copper print. Artist unknown.

Page 21   *Portrait of William Kent*. Oil on canvas. Artist unknown.
          Portrait of Lord Burlington. Artist unknown.
          Royal occasion in colonial India. Watercolour. G. Amato.

Page 22   *Chiswick House, Middlesex*. Oil on canvas. Artist unknown.
          Portrait of Sir William Chambers. Oil. Richard Houston.
          View of Westminster from Adelphi Terrace. Oil on canvas.
          Artist unknown.

Page 23   *The Adam brothers*. Oil on canvas. Artist unknown.

Page 24   *Opening of Parliament in the reign of Queen Victoria*.
          Woodprint. Artist unknown.
          Portrait of Sir John Nash. Oil on canvas. Artist unknown.

Page 25   *View of Regent's Park from Primrose Hill*. Oil on canvas. John Knox.
          Portrait of Queen Victoria. Oil. Alexander de Malvilla.
          Crystal Palace. Steel print. Artist unknown.

Page 26   *Portrait of Charles Barry*. Oil. Artist unknown.
          Illustration of Oliver Twist, 10th chapter. Lithograph. George Cruickshank.
          Victoria Station. Oil. Eugenio Álvarez.

Page 27   *Victoria Embankment*. Photograph. Photographer unknown.

Page 28   *Victoria and Albert Museum*. Postcard. Artist unknown.
          Staircase in a London subway station. Photograph.
          Artist unknown.
          Cover of Gropius Bauhaus Bauten Dessau. Illustration.
          Lázlo Moholy-Nagy.

Page 29   *Bombing in front of the Bank of England*. Photograph. Photographer
          unknown.
          Greater London Region Plan.
          Panoramic view of London at the end of the 1950s.

Page 30   Festival of Britain. Poster illustration. Artist unknown.
          Queen Elizabeth II. Photograph. Photographer unknown.
          Ronan Point building after its collapse.
          Photographer. Photographer unknown.

Page 31   Interior of Covent Garden. Photograph. Photographer unknown.

Page 32   View of the housing built in the Docklands.
          Photograph. Photographer unknown.
          Panoramic view of London in the 1980s.
          Photograph. Photographer unknown.
          Richard Rogers. Photographic portrait. Artist unknown.

Page 33   Charles, Prince of Wales. Photograph. Photographer unknown.
          Millennium Bridge. Photograph. Photographer unknown.
          Portrait of Sir. Norman Foster. Photograph. Photographer unknown.

Page 34   Panoramic view of the Docklands in the 1990s. Photograph. Photographer
          unknown.
          Panoramic view of London in the future. Photomontage. Artist unknown.
          Future venue for the 2012 Olympic Games. Photomontage.
          Artist unknown.

Page 35   Panoramic view of the Docklands in the future. Photomontage. Artist
          unknown.
          View of the city from the London Eye. Photograph. Inge Clemente.

Page 40   View of an old map of London. Copper print.
          Artist unknown.
          Map of London. Copper print. Artist unknown.

Page 42   Panoramic view of London in the reign of Elizabeth I.
          Copper print. Artist unknown.